GENTLY LEAD

Also by Polly Berrien Berends

Whole Child/Whole Parent
Coming to Life

GENTLY LEAD

HOW TO TEACH

YOUR CHILDREN

ABOUT GOD

WHILE FINDING OUT

FOR YOURSELF

New Revised Edition

Polly Berrien Berends

A Crossroad Book
The Crossroad Publishing Company
New York

1998

The Crossroad Publishing Company
370 Lexington Avenue, New York, NY 10017

Grateful acknowledgment is made for permission to reprint the following:

"Woods" from *Clearing* by Wendell Berry. Copyright © 1977, 1975, 1974 by Wendell
Berry. Reprinted by permission of Harcourt Brace Jovanovich, Inc.

An excerpt from "Wild Geese" from *The Country of Marriage* by Wendell Berry.
Copyright © 1973, 1972, 1971 by Wendell Berry. Reprinted by permission of Harcourt Brace Jovanovich, Inc.

Untitled poem from *Knee Deep in Thunder* by Sheila Moon. Copyright © 1967 by
Sheila Moon. Reprinted with the permission of the Guild for Psychological Studies
Publishing House.

Designed by Alma Orenstein

Printed in the United States of America

Library of Congress Cataloging-in-Publication Data

Berends, Polly Berrien.
    Gently Lead : how to teach your children about God while finding
out for yourself / [Polly Berrien Berends].— New rev. ed.
        p.   cm.
    ISBN 0–8245–1733–4 (pbk.)
    1. Religious education of children.   2. Children—Religious life.
I. Title.
BL42.B47   1998
291.4'41—dc21   97–49001
                                                            CIP

He shall feed his flock like a shepherd,
and gently lead them that are with young.

—Isa. 40:11

To, by, for
my beloved sons and teachers
and fellow children of God
Jan Berrien and Andrew Lukas

CONTENTS

INTRODUCTION TO THE REVISED EDITION   *xv*

ONCE UPON A TIME   *1*

TAKING IT AS IT COMES   *5*

Now Is the Time, This Is the Place   *6*
Day by Day   *13*
Adviser of Advisers   *14*

GOD   *17*

A Secret   *18*
I Spy   *19*
Gravity   *20*
Angels in Charge   *22*

SPIRITUAL SEEING   *23*

Snowflake   *24*
Thought for Food   *26*
It Takes One to Know One   *27*
Itchy   *28*
God's Eye View   *30*

Seeing in the Dark   *31*
Fear Not Said He for Mighty Dread   *32*
Lemon Aid   *34*

WHO'S WHO   *37*

Who Does God Think We Are?   *38*
Should Fit   *39*
Who Do You Think You Are?   *40*
Holy Christmas   *41*
The Star Child   *42*
Born Again   *45*
Dear Walter   *47*
Who Did They Think He Was?   *48*
Not Too Carefully Taught   *49*

WHAT'S WHAT   *53*

Before Ye Ask   *54*
No Exceptions   *56*
Afloat and Afraid   *58*
Unhugs   *60*
Love   *62*

QUIET SEEING   *63*

Finding a Footing   *64*
Side by Side   *66*
Is Anything Too Hard?   *68*
Grace   *70*
Bed and Board   *72*
Bedtime Prayer   *73*
Amen   *74*
In the Beginning Is the Word   *75*

WHAT DIES AND WHAT DOESN'T   *81*

Death of a Pet   *82*
Coming and Going   *83*
Good-Bye   *84*
Hello   *85*
Outgrowing   *86*
Changing Shape   *87*
Cemetery   *88*
Santa Claus   *91*
God's Child   *92*

THE HUMDRUM IS THE HOLY   *93*

Today Is the Day   *94*
Boredom   *95*
Fetching and Chopping   *97*
. . . And Raking   *99*

GOING FORTH WITH JOY   *101*

Now and Forever   *102*
All Things Bright and Beautiful   *104*
Not Even a Mouse   *105*
Geese Overhead   *108*
Who Did You Say?   *110*
After You   *111*
The Green and Gracious Dragon   *113*
The Pathmaker   *115*
Grandmother   *117*

LOVE THINE ENEMY   *119*

Anthill   *120*
The Enemy   *122*

All Things   *124*
What a Laugh   *125*
Halloween Mask   *126*
Toad   *127*
The Only I Am in the World   *128*
The Peacemaker   *129*

TOUGH MOMENTS   *131*

It's Not Easy Being Green   *132*
Twenty-third Psalm   *135*
Angry   *137*
Hard Things   *139*
Leave Odd Things Where You Find Them   *140*

THE GOD OF ALL CREATIVITY   *143*

Pen and Whistle   *144*
A Good Idea   *145*
How to Get Gifts from an Elephant   *146*
Christmas Elf   *150*
Divine Mathematics   *152*
Okra   *153*

WORSHIP   *155*

Too Sad   *156*
Going to Search   *159*

A DIEU   *161*

Martin   *162*
The Runaway Bunny   *165*
What Changes and What Doesn't   *167*
Who Called?   *168*
Holy Moses   *169*

INTRODUCTION TO THE REVISED EDITION

This book largely wrote itself as I lived with my children and tried to see what ideas of God or higher power, prayer, and spirit had to do with our everyday lives. Besides wanting to give my sons a spiritual footing, being a parent deepened my awareness of the need to rely on a greater, more reliable Beyond Personal source of love, guidance, and support than myself or my husband. I saw that our whole journey was basically a spiritual awakening. I taught the children what they forced me to learn. And, of course, they taught me.

Very early in life certain mishaps began my conscious spiritual quest for something Beyond Personal to count on. I first found it in the woods and fields near which, no matter where we moved, I was blessed to live. When I felt lonely in the world, in the wild I found myself unlonely. If I felt like a misfit, in the wild I knew I fit in. As we moved from one strange place to another, in each new woods I felt at once at home. There, when my world seemed to fall apart, I felt something undergirding. There, when bad feelings made me feel like a bad person I found freedom from judgment. When upset, by brooks and ponds I felt peace bubble up. In lacy ferns, trees, and creatures great and small, I saw signs, felt the presence, of an underlying intelligence and order wherein even incomprehensible death and destruction seemed part of a meticulous, beautiful, even loving presence that could be trusted. In the wild I found a source and force of guidance and love that eventually I called God.

At age seven I took myself to church. There I met not only my familiar Beyond Personal "God of all creation," in which, as Paul said, "we live and move and have our being . . . who is before all things and in whom all things consist," but also a highly personal one, who fed Jonah to a whale and helped chosen people to slay others. Besides the surrounding, upholding, and holding presence I knew, here was a lofty, remote, tempermental father who killed his son, who knew when I was bad or good, and who would one day send me to heaven or hell accordingly (and I knew which), who was altogether too much like the father from whose wrath I sometimes fled to the woods. This God seemed unbelievable, meaningless, irrelevant, dreadful. Yet church fellowship, music, psalms, and ritual drew me. An innate sense of oneness and my longing to belong among persons as I did in the wild moved me to seek deeper connection between my nonpersonal wilderness and the interpersonal world, between my Beyond Personal God and the personal God of traditional JudeoChristianity.

As the Age of Reason divided reason from emotion, body from soul, matter from spirit, science from religion, exalting the former as truth above the latter as mere illusion, many found it harder to believe in traditional Western religion. Into the breach dove depth psychology, especially Jungian, which, by plumbing the unconscious, uncovered layers of reality and self wherein footing for a "union of opposites" could be found. Western religion largely clung to the old, deteriorating in many ways to codified beliefs and strictures. For me, study of psyche and psychotherapy helped clarify what I missed in organized religion. Study of Eastern religions and theologians Eckhart, Tillich, and Buber helped me to see that what I missed in Western preaching and practice was—and had always been—in our scriptures and rituals and lay waiting to be uncovered and rediscovered for our time. In college, seminary, and adulthood, my participation in church fluctuated according to my need, understanding, and patience. But I continued off-trail, finding links between psyche, soma, and spirit, and between the two Gods and two worlds of my childhood that afforded sounder psychospiritual footing.

Parenthood took me further. I saw that to a child, so newly emerged from oneness with the whole, the idea of God comes easily. I saw that to a child, whose first source of life support, wisdom, and love is personal, the idea of a God in the image of a parent comes easily. I saw that to a child, weaned from personal umbilical, breast, and arms, to direct reliance on the environment for air, food, and support, the idea of God as "that in which we live and move and have our being" also comes easily. I saw that, for children, the transition from one idea of God to the other can be smooth, that to them there is no conflict between the idea of a personal God and a Beyond Personal one. In my own growth I saw that life is an endless series of weanings from reliance on personally mediated support to ever-deeper direct reliance on ever-deeper layers of Beyond Personal support. I saw that the psychospiritual weanings and stages of adulthood are directly parallel to and accomplished in the same way as the psychophysical weanings and stages of childhood. I saw that as teenagers must psychologically wean themselves from their parents, the last centuries of Western culture are not the end of religion but weaning to broader, deeper, more direct spiritual awakening to the Beyond Personal, which underlies all of its manifestations and channels. I saw how the personal, interpersonal, and nonpersonal are nested in Beyond Personal.

When he first went off to college, one of our sons lived with other freshmen who like him were living unsupervised for the first time and going overboard. He found he had something unique to go on. It wasn't so much that he wasn't tempted to get into trouble as that he understood how to get out of it. "I'm noticing," he said, "that I have something others don't. I'm pretty sure it's the spiritual way of looking at life you taught us. I don't know how anyone can live without it." As a parent I couldn't have lived without a spiritual perspective. It may not have made me a better parent or more of a parent. The best thing it did was to make for *less* parent. It allowed me to look at parenthood as a learning process, to forgive myself, and to go on. It somewhat protected my sons *from* me by opening doors, windows and ceilings to the Parent beyond us to which each of us could turn.

So, as I sought to help my children find a spiritual foundation and footing in it, my own spiritual foundation and footing grew. Bewildering sorrow, fear, failures, and fits that dragged us down as well as the mysterious beauty, joy, and love that uplifted us, deepened my understanding of prayer and kept me at it. A better subtitle for *Gently Lead* than *How To Teach Your Children About God **While** Finding Out for Yourself* would be *How To Teach Your Children About God **By** Finding Out for Yourself,* for clearly the best way my children learned from me about God was not from my spoken knowledge and teaching but from my silent, prayerful, *un*knowing listening and groping. Space does not permit me to add many things to this book which, looking back, I now recall, nor to amplify what is stated briefly here. More can be found in my *Coming to Life* and in the revised fourth edition of *Whole Child/Whole Parent* (especially the new introduction and "Additional Reflections" listed in its index).

I didn't write *Gently Lead* to tell others what to teach their children, but to share my own discovery of what a rich, mutual spiritual journey our ordinary, everyday lives are. I tried to present a spiritual perspective from which I hope others, whether in or out of organized religion, may discover and share with children this dimension of dimensions. This is an anecdotal record of some of our spiritual experiments and findings, the best of which often arose when we were at our worst. Lest anyone feel envious, as if we did right what others do wrong or fail to do, it is worth noting that, of all my adult books, this is the thinnest. I hope you'll listen more *through* than *to* it, and not make the mistake of trying to say or do in your unique situations what came to us in ours. There is no right way or doctrine. We each start from where we are, taking next steps with our children, more as fellow children of God than as their parents.

—P.B.B., 1997

ONCE UPON
A TIME

I had been conducting seminars, counseling counselees, writing writings, doing dishes, and folding underpants almost simultaneously for years. All things are possible—that was my lesson. Suddenly an opportunity arose for my children to vacation with family in Holland, where there were caring, overseeing grandparents, uncles, and cousins galore. What a thing to let them go! What an opportunity for them—and for me!

Your children change you so much. They change you for the good and they change you for good. But what *would* life be like when someday they would be gone? I had wondered that. What will I be like? Who am I without them? Now I would have a chance to see.

The boys left, and I didn't die! Seminars ceased for the summer. Clients left on vacation. Amazing peace fell. It was a dramatic silence. I was aware of not having arranged it. Things had simply fallen into place. Within two weeks everything came to a halt, like the moment before the conductor taps the baton. For one week I cleaned house, tuning up. I listened for the tapping, looked to see when to begin what.

Then came a lovely invitation to Vermont. The invitation was for me alone. Not even my husband was invited. It seemed almost too luxurious—a private vacation, beautiful surroundings, and a dear friend for a hostess. Feeling like a kid going to camp, I went, with folders of started manuscripts, scraps of this and that, tossed into the trunk of the car at the last minute.

Never, not since I was six in summer, had a day been so long as those few. I felt like Ezekiel, who always talks about God standing him up on his feet and putting him someplace, like a chess piece, for some reason. Late at night were moonlit fields to walk in, so quiet and so empty that, standing there, it seemed we were the only ones on our big planet—like the Little Prince on his tiny one, sticking up in space. But in the morning at five o'clock the birds sang, lifting me, like clean sheet to clothesline, to behold the sunrise and Mount Ascutney—and then to type. Two or three weeks, twice to Vermont for two or three days at a time, and a manuscript was done. Immediately word came of the boys' return flight. No time at all to wonder—only to count the minutes until their arrival and to rejoice.

That was years ago, ten to be exact. They were seven and nine years old then. Now they are seventeen and nineteen. One is in college. The other is almost out of high school. What I took a vacation from that summer is almost over. At the moment I am again trying on my life beyond parenthood, only this time it is not an experiment, it is for real. I am all alone, for a whole month, in New Hampshire, in a lovely cabin by a lovely lake, reorienting by writing. Two weeks are already past. I have completed revisions on another book and am ready to return to this one begun so long ago. I meant to publish it before now, but other things interfered. Daily life, mostly. So *Gently Lead* stayed quietly put aside. I think it is because it wasn't finished. It couldn't be finished until I was.

Yesterday I finally saw a loon. I'm sure it was a female on a break from her brood because she didn't seem to be feeding or going any place in particular. She just sort of kept turning around and looking about as if to say, *Am I really alone?* and *Is it really all right? Do I love it?* or *Do I hate it?* I could identify with that.

Then she did something so funny. She was quite nearby and with binoculars I had a wonderfully clear look at her. Well, you know how mysterious and staid loons are. You never see them exerting any effort to swim. They seem to glide as if nothing at all is going on beneath the surface and they are just having a ride. Well, all of a sudden, out from behind her tail feathers, up comes her huge black webbed foot, which gets flapped and waved vigorously about in the air for a moment, before disappearing again. And we are talking about *huge* black feet here (you don't swim fifty yards underwater with little dainty ones). A moment later, *flip*, up comes the other one to be flapped frivolously in the air as well. *Shake it, Mama,* I thought. All this time her front end is looking just as dignified and mysterious as ever, as if she didn't know anything at all about the frivolous funny business going on in back. I don't think she saw me, but I certainly felt I knew who I was looking at.

To write this book I have reached backward in time to where my own two feet have trod. We can be too serious about our importance as parents sometimes, heavy-handed and -footed in the bargain. Somebody said angels are just people who take themselves lightly. I hope this backward look makes it easier for some families to take things more lightly —through prayer, to laugh more often.

—P.B.B., 1989

TAKING IT
AS IT COMES

NOW IS THE TIME, THIS IS THE PLACE

If there is one thing I have learned from these years, it is that it is not only okay but actually good to take life as it comes. With notably regrettable exceptions, this is what I have done, but I have not always felt confident that I was doing the right thing. I hope that hearing from me will make some people feel easier about yielding to the spiritual opportunities of parenthood. I had originally intended to open *Gently Lead* with a little piece called "Zen Mom," which included a dream I dreamed and a dialogue I had with my sons. Instead I used it to open the revised edition of *Whole Child/Whole Parent*, but I repeat the dream and the dialogue here as an illustration of the point that it is good to take life as it comes, because it will all add up. First of all the dream.

Once I had a dream. In the dream I was to receive a diploma certifying my readiness to be a spiritual teacher or guide of some sort. There were two of us being presented with a certificate. The other diplomate was a man. He was Swamibabgururishiroshirabbisoandso. He wore long colorful robes and had a fistful of degrees and certificates. To receive his diploma it was only necessary to present himself with his long titles, flowing robes, and abundant credentials. But before me there stood an enormous mountain of laundry. Evidently to receive my diploma I would first have to climb over this huge heap of laundry.

So, you see the conflict. It was just the beginning of women's lib. We were hard up financially, and I was frequently tempted to think that our financial security depended on my leaving the children to go back to school for additional training.

Or else I should forget about writing and counseling, which always had to be squeezed in around the edges, and do something more practical. But I never seemed to be able to do that. Restless though I sometimes felt, I didn't want to leave the children—less because I thought they needed me than because I didn't want to miss out. To go to school would have been expensive; daily living was costly enough. And where would I study? I couldn't seem to find any place that would teach me a truly spiritual approach to counseling, and to study more traditional approaches felt like a U-turn. To stop writing and counseling around the edges, either for school or for something more practical, also didn't seem right. The dream suggested that for the time being my school, my research frontier, my path to fulfillment, my work for now, was the rather traditional woman's life before me, and *that it would add up*. It was not an envious dream, just a worried one. It reflected my conviction, the choice I made, *and* the doubts I had about it. But now I can truthfully say that it has added up. The dialogue I had with my sons completes this picture.

CHILD: Mom, how did you get to know so much about God?

MOTHER: I don't know much. But I've been around for a while and been to schools and had wonderful teachers. There were teachers from the past, too—Moses and Isaiah and Jesus and Buddha. But besides all those, I have two private Zen masters who are always teaching me and making my learning into real understanding and love. I am very very grateful for these two private Zen masters.

CHILDREN: Tell us! Who are they? What are their names? You never told us about them!

MOTHER: Their names are Jan and Andy. It is you who are my Zen masters.

CHILDREN (*laughing*): Oh, Mom! We teach *you?* You're joking.

MOTHER: No, I am not kidding. You are my two best Zen masters.

That remains true to this day. As I have spelled out more fully in *Whole Child/Whole Parent,* the real parents of our children are the ideas that govern us. Most are notions from the past about who we are and what is important in life. We are not aware of most of these ideas or that they are troublesome and mistaken. So they cling to us and we cling to them, like non-swimmers to twigs, heading over the falls. These same ideas become parents of our children. Our children become the spitting (and sometimes kicking and biting) images of these ideas, which prove painfully false in their lives just as in ours. The more we suffer, and especially the more we see our children suffer, the more open-minded we become. If we look for the ideas behind their behavior we can discover just what ideas are running our lives. In this way, our children raise us at least as much as we raise them. The result is an unprecedented opportunity to discover the real parent of both ourselves and our children, to become conscious children of God. This can only happen if we approach parenthood for learning. When we try to master parenthood or to master our children we just stay stuck and hurt each other. But when we let our children be our Zen masters and approach problems and failures as something to learn from, parenthood becomes a joyful, fruitful grope.

So *Gently Lead* is truly about teaching your children about God by finding out for yourself, because so much of what they learn about God will be from watching you try to find out for yourself. Jesus said, "Seek and ye shall find." Your children will not always do what you tell them to do, but they will be—good and bad—as they see you being. If your children see you seeking they will seek—the finding part is up to God.

When I was a child we used to stretch out on the floor on Sundays and read the funnies. By the time my children came along I had developed the habit of turning frequently to the Bible—not religiously and not necessarily on Sundays, but daily and often, for understanding to live by. I open the Bible the way you check your mailbox, to see if there is a message for me. So my sons grew up seeing this, and when they were five or six I was very surprised when I suddenly began to find them stretched out on the floor and reading, not the funnies, but the Bible! They searched out passages from *Godspell* or the real story of Daniel, or, as if on a treasure hunt, tracked down the one special place in that huge book where the Twenty-third Psalm is located. I never told them to read the Bible or suggested that they should, but they caught the interest as children catch colds.

It is not uncommon for parents to find their thoughts running Godward. Said one parent, "I was raised in the church and went to Sunday school. I stopped going years ago, and I know I could never go back to the way I was taught. But now that I have children, I am wondering . . ." This book is for you. You may have picked it up because you want to teach your children about God. More likely you have tried and ruled out the possibility that you yourself are your child's God, creator, and ruler, and you are looking for outside help. But let's face facts. Who's rearing whom? Isn't it our children who are teaching us about God? The Bible says, "And a little child shall lead them." Drive them is more like it.

It is a little known fact that the real business of parenthood is the upbringing of the parent. Children will value what we value and rely on what we rely on. So beware. Be aware. Don't look for much technique in these pages. This is not a method. It is a catalog of surprising moments intended only to demonstrate the possibilities of God-reliant parenthood, in which it is seen that God is the parent, and both parent and child are God's children.

The little we teach our children about God is almost a side issue. In a way the less said about God, the better. And then it must not be religious, or the children will find God irrelevant. It must not be preachy, or the children will find God trivial. It must not be "should-ful" or they will resist, rebel, and reject. Let God be God's idea, occurring spontaneously and responsively to you and your children together.

It must be reiterated that our family life was not exceptional. Much of our life together was less than nothing to write home about, let alone to be bookworthy. Recorded here are exceptional moments in ordinary lives—rare, spontaneous ones arising not out of great knowledge, but great ignorance. Through the willingness to be vastly, desperately ignorant, we become receptive to sudden inspired wisdom. First we are willing to be powerless, then we become more sincere; then God comes. "Except ye become as little children, ye shall never enter the kingdom of heaven." They forgot to mention that it is the children who would make plain our powerlessness to us.

Our native desire for love leads us toward God. It manifests itself as a desire to trust. Where we let our children down and are forced to admit that on our own we cannot fail to fail, there comes again this cry for something to trust. We find many ways to deny or sedate this urge, but then along come our children *trusting us!* Oh, God.

Why bring God into this? Why complicate things? We've got each other—what more is there? But whether you call it Higher Power or Order of Being or Fundamental Mind or

One Mind or Our Father or Our Mother or Life, the fact is that God is the only truly simplifying factor. It is trying to live without God that is so complicated and hard. Having children, having each other may not be turning out to be as terrific as we imagined. Somehow someone is always feeling had. Jesus saw this. He said, "a man's foes will be those of his own household" (Matt. 10:36).

So, loving them, we grow. Partly we want so badly for it to be good for them, to renovate our own childhoods, and to prove ourselves to our parents (actual or at large, interior or exterior, dead, alive, or imaginary). Also, we don't want to let this opportunity of family life drift by just coping and hanging in there without receiving the blessing we know is there. So, awed by the beauty and goodness of our children, dumbfounded by our failure to be the parents we hoped to be, worshipping, giving horsey rides, and picking up peas, we are brought to our knees. It's a good idea to learn to pray. "Now I lay me down"—not "to sleep," but to *wake*. Physicist David Bohm speaks of "psychological atom smashing." As the atom is smashed to release tremendous physical energy, so through prayer we smash the limits of personal power for good and ill. And, lo and behold, right here at home we can see it—all heaven breaking loose!

> And the Spirit of the Lord shall rest upon him, the spirit of wisdom and understanding, the spirit of counsel and might, the spirit of knowledge and the fear of the Lord. And shall make him quick of understanding in the fear of the Lord. He shall not judge by what his eyes see, or decide by what his ears hear, but with righteousness shall he judge. . . . The wolf shall dwell with the lamb, and the leopard shall lie down with the kid; and the calf and the young lion and the fatling together; and a little child shall lead them. And the cow and the bear shall feed; their

young shall lie down together; and the lion shall eat
straw like the ox. The sucking child shall play on the hole
of the asp, and the weaned child shall put his hand on
the adder's den. They shall not hurt nor destroy on all
my holy mountain; for the earth shall be full of the
knowledge of the Lord, as the waters cover the sea.

—Isa. 11:2–9

DAY BY DAY

Day by day.
Day by day.
Oh, dear Lord,
three things I pray—
To see Thee more clearly.
Love Thee more dearly,
Follow Thee more nearly,
Day by day.

—Richard of Chichester, ca. 1197–1253

That says it all, doesn't it? It is an outstanding creed for living.
A creed for parents. A creed for children. A creed for families.
And the whole instruction book.

ADVISER OF ADVISERS

Call #1

SON: Hi, Mom!

PARENT: Hi! What's new?

SON: I didn't get the adviser I wanted for my religion major.

PARENT: Professor Z—— said no? That's too bad. How come? Your friend got him, didn't she?

SON: Yes, but she asked him last semester. He's on leave this semester. He's here and will advise his existing advisees, but he won't take on any new ones.

PARENT: Oh, too bad. You must be disappointed. What about next semester? Will he do it then?

SON: I think so, but I figure maybe it just wasn't meant to be. I'm going to ask Professor W—— instead.

Call #2

SON: Hi! Guess what? I got my religion adviser.

PARENT: Great! Who is it? Professor W——?

SON: Nope, that's why I called. You won't believe this. For some reason I never gave Professor W—— the adviser's form. I don't know why. But I just kept not doing it.

PARENT: You were still wishing to have Professor Z——?

SON: Not really. When that didn't work out I kept thinking I'm just going to wait to see what God has in mind, if you know what I mean.

PARENT: Yes! Good! So what happened?

SON: Today I was walking across campus, and I saw Professor L——. Remember? I had him last year? He taught myth and ritual, which is my favorite course so far. So he sees me and waves me over. He said, "Hey, I haven't seen you in a long time. How are you doing? I don't remember your name, but you were one of my favorite students last year. Are you going to major in religion by any chance?" I tell him that I am, and he says, "That's great! May I be your adviser?" Isn't that beautiful?

PARENT: It sure is!

GOD

A SECRET

Here's a secret:
God means good.
It's a secret
because you can't see it
or taste it or touch it.
But you can know it
and show it.

I wanted to introduce the boys to God as a source of love and
wisdom beyond self and other. I tried to teach them that God
is a reliable force, not a temperamental person like Mom and
Dad. We used personal pronouns for God, because a child's
concept of love is legitimately personal. But we also tried to
convey the idea that God is a force that is always present, at
all times and in all places. I also tried to help them understand
that God is spirit. God's nature is invisible good—love, peace,
intelligence—which they could see with an inner seeing and
thereby bring to light in their lives. We looked to find this God
in everyone and underlying everything. I tried to help them
become aware of their ability to see and be inspired in this
spiritual way. I tried to help them discover that this God is the
source and force behind their lives.

I SPY

Dear Lord, I spy
with my secret eye
something invisible!
Something that can't be touched
or tasted or heard,
Something that never ends.
I spy with my secret eye
what is lovely
and lasting
and true.
I spy with my secret eye—
I spy *you!*

GRAVITY

PARENT: How do you walk?

CHILD: I stand up and put one foot in front of the other.

PARENT: Yes, but what happens if you lean too far over?

CHILD: I fall down.

PARENT: Why?

CHILD: The law of gravity. If I'm not balanced gravity pulls me down.

PARENT: Right! So it's important to stay lined up with the law of gravity, isn't it?

CHILD: Yeah! Because then it helps me. I saw a show about astronauts in space. You couldn't walk without gravity. You would just float away and bump into things.

PARENT: God is like gravity. We need to stay in touch with God. If we do, then God helps us to live, just the way the law of gravity helps us to walk. It's always there to help us if we stay in touch. But if we don't stay in touch we get lost and hurt.

CHILD: How do we stay in touch with God?

PARENT: That's a big question. It takes a special kind of listening. You have to get very quiet inside and listen.

CHILD: Will I hear God talk out loud?

PARENT: Probably not. But you will get ideas—very good ones whenever you need them. Or peace will come and you won't feel scared about something. You know how we have quiet times—like when we sit still for a minute before we talk about something? And we take time for prayer every day?

CHILD: Yes, and when I have a problem sometimes we read something? I like when we do that.

PARENT: Me, too. Those are all ways of getting in touch with God. We listen and wait for God to guide us.

CHILD: In *Star Wars* they always say, "May the Force be with you." I guess they mean God, don't you?

PARENT: Yes.

CHILD: It would make more sense to say, "May you be with the Force."

ANGELS IN CHARGE

For he will give his angels charge over [them], to keep [them] in all [their] ways.
On their hands shall they bear [them] up, lest [they] dash [their] foot against a stone.

—Ps. 91

I don't believe that the Force would have caught on with my children if it hadn't caught on with me. When I was overanxious and fearful for my children I contributed nothing but stress, pressure, fear, and anger to any situation. I found it helpful to prayerfully relieve myself of personal responsibility by considering such writings as this psalm. Sometimes I substituted *them* (meaning the children) for *thee* throughout. It helped me to get out from between my children and God. The less forceful I thought I had to be, the easier it was to let the Godforce through—to the children and to me. Giving even the idea of God charge over my consciousness for even a moment seemed to help.

Generally speaking the first step in any trouble is to seek peace. As I look back I think that a tolerance for and love of private peaceful times was one of the two most valuable things the children learned—the other, of course, was that there was something beyond us both to be turned to and counted on. How many times we said it, "Let's first get still," "find peace," "take time," "and then we'll see."

SPIRITUAL SEEING

SNOWFLAKE

How many ways
can you find God
in
a
snowflake?

cold
white
tiny
melts
beauty
uniqueness
peace
perfection
purity
?

This was just a little exercise to cultivate spiritual consciousness. The idea is to pick out the spiritual qualities, that is, the
aspects of a snowflake that also describe God and God's good.
Cold, white, and melts, of course, are material traits experi-
enced through the senses. Beauty, uniqueness, peace, perfection, and purity are spiritual qualities, spiritually discerned.

> For we look not on the things that are seen, but on the
> things that are not seen. For the things that are seen are
> of the flesh, and the things that are unseen are of the
> spirit.
>
> —2 Cor. 4:18

How silently, how silently
the wondrous gift is given.

So God imparts through human hearts
the blessings of his heaven.

—"O Little Town of Bethlehem"

God is Spirit, and they that worship him must worship
him in spirit and in truth.

—John 4:24

THOUGHT FOR FOOD

. . . whatsoever things are true, whatsoever things are
honest, whatsoever things are just, whatsoever things are
pure, whatsoever things are lovely, whatsoever things are
of good report; if there be any virtue, and if there be any
praise, think on these things.

—Phil. 4:8

As a child, I went to a wonderful summer camp. After meals,
along with announcements, the head counselor always read
something inspiring—sometimes from the Bible, sometimes
not. This last passage was often read, and it inspired me, so
I gave it to my children. Bible reading at mealtime can be
wonderful. My husband grew up in Holland. An important
part of every meal and the primary way he learned what was
in the Bible was when his father read from the Bible at mealtime. We tried this in fits and starts, but for some reason it
never became a regular habit. The right spirit has to be there,
and it wasn't. If I had it to do over I would hope this could
work out. It is such an efficient way to provide exposure to the
Bible, and so wholesome for a family to share not only food
for the body but also food for thought, thought for food. But
you can't insist on it. The right spirit has to be there.

IT TAKES ONE TO KNOW ONE

Your child is distressed, cranky, fussy, upset, and a pain in the neck today, and you would like to get rid of her—

Your child is going away for the first time, and you already miss her. You would like to keep her young and beside you forever—

Your child seems frightened, apathetic, troubled, and you are worried that there is something really wrong, damaged, or messed up—

How many ways can you see God in your child? Blond? Angry? Nice? Lively? Graceful? Intelligent? Spontaneous? Messy? Orderly? Joyful? Peaceful? Can you distinguish who she really is from who she really isn't? Can you recognize spiritual qualities in your child that you can be aware of even when you can't see or hear or touch him? How many better things do you have to do right now than to give joy, bring peace, discover what use God has for you, discover God, learn what it means to walk in love, set another free?

ITCHY

CHILD: I have this itch on my knee. It's bothering me. I can't get to sleep with all this itching.

PARENT: Well, it's time for prayers now. Maybe if you can stop thinking about it you won't notice it. Try thinking about something else.

CHILD: But I can't stop thinking about it. It itches! How can you think of something else if you itch?

PARENT: Well, you just can't have your mind on two things at the same time. Try this. I'm going to say something, and you try to think about your itch. Don't think about what I'm saying.

CHILD *(giggling)*: This is gonna be fun.

PARENT *(loudly, deliberately, with dramatic expression)*: Ninety-two. Ninety-two. Ninety-two. Ninety-two. Ninety-two. Okay, what were you thinking about?

CHILD: Ninety-two! I couldn't help it. But now I'm itching again. I can't keep thinking ninety-two all night.

PARENT: Okay. Now suppose you try to think of God. If you could do that there would be no more itching.

CHILD: That's hard. I don't know how.

PARENT: Well, let's try this. How many ways can you see God in a snowflake? Is God white and cold?

CHILD: No. I get it! I already know God is spiritual. That means you can't see it or feel it. God is pure. Right?

PARENT: Yes.

CHILD *(interested)*: And peace? And beauty? And every snowflake is different. Right?

PARENT: Yes, uniqueness is a spiritual quality. Very good.

CHILD: The itch *is* gone! I can even think about it, but it isn't there.

PARENT: Wonderful. And the best part is that now you know how to put your mind on God. How many ways can you see God in a butterfly? Think about it and tell me in the morning. Okay?

CHILD: Oh boy. This is going to be fun. Good night, Mom. Would you go now so I can start?

GOD'S EYE VIEW

How many ways
can you find God
in
you
?
intelligence
love
beauty
joy
freedom
peace
ticklish
blue eyes
wears jeans
?

SEEING IN THE DARK

The lights are off.
It's dark in my room.
And I am imagining *things.*
I imagine I'm all alone
in a room full of eyes and
spies and beasts and bad guys.
That's what I imagine.
But then I remember
my room is too full
for all that stuff.
It's full to the brim
with love.
That's what's nice about the dark, God.
In the dark I cannot see
my daytime toys.
I need not see my nighttime *things*
But in the dark at bedtime, God,
I see you.

FEAR NOT SAID HE FOR
MIGHTY DREAD

Bedtime can be a crisis time—a time for terror or for power struggle. If there is angry interaction in the home, even when it is not directed at the child, there can be nightmares and fear at night. I was horrified when one of my children repeatedly dreamed of a certain monster, which he called the Mommit. There was a friend who used to bully him a bit. His last name was Pittman, and there came the other monster to fear at night. For a time the poor child was haunted in his sleep by both the Mommit and the Pit! Perhaps we made monstrous demands on him to be nice or a little man and a sport, thus trapping him between two feared and resented monsters. He denies that the Mommit was me and says the Pit was named for the sound it made—*ptt ptt pttt*—like a crab bubbling. But I wonder. I was pretty crabby at times.

Learning to pray can help your child begin to learn to deal with such fears. First listen. Listen and comfort. You need to understand what the fears are, and your child needs to know that her fears are understandable—not something the matter with her. Then you can pray together, opening your minds to a source of light and reassurance. Yes, parents need to pray too, because our children's fears, which are often of *our* monsters, may be too big for her prayers.

So you as parents need to pray your heads empty of powerful monsters, too. There is the little monster who "won't let me have a minute to myself." This very dear little monster needs to know that she is loved at all times, which depends on your knowing that she is not just an interruption in your career or marriage or pleasure but a wonderful, worthy, learning individual. This little monster also needs to know that you are not the only source of love in her life, which depends on you not depending on her to make you feel like the most important person on earth. There are our big monsters, too, what we ourselves fear—not being accepted, being blamed, making mistakes, not looking good, an angry spouse, loneliness. The same monsters that we worship and run from by day chase our children at night. So pray with your children, whether at their bedsides or in the next room. Pray away the monsters.

Not all nightmares should be sent packing for good —only for the rest of the night so your child can sleep in peace. What I didn't know when my children were small is that most dream figures represent unconscious energies, feelings, and parts of the dreamer's own personality. They may seem scary and monstrous merely because they are so unfamiliar or so full of energy. They may take fierce angry form because they are frustrated and need attention. Or perhaps your child has inferred that certain feelings and parts of herself are dangerous because her parents don't like them. See suggestions in *Whole Child/Whole Parent* (1997 edition) for helping children explore and befriend dream creatures in the safe light of day.

LEMON AID

There was a father who loved plants.
There was a yellow-eyed cat who chewed plants.
The father became extremely angry
and used a lot of foul language at the cat
and threatened to get rid of her one way or another.

There was a mother who feared
the effect of foul language on their five-year-old child.
She asked the father to calm down and not swear.
The father grew even angrier
and used foul language at the mother
and threatened to leave.

The mother got scared and saw that she had no power to
overpower
the father's feelings of powerlessness.
So she shut up and prayed.

She remembered that the only real power
over her child was God.
She remembered that as light overcomes darkness
and darkness cannot overcome light
so God can overcome all evil.
She considered that therefore
she did not have to fight against
bad influence and fear.

Suddenly the child spoke up.
"Hey, Dad, I've got an idea!
Maybe the reason Lemon eats plants
Is because we don't love her enough.

Maybe if we love her more
she will stop bothering the plants."
The father smiled and hugged the child.
"You know what?" he said, patting the cat.
"I bet you're right."

Children can be inspired directly if the parents get out of the way. Give God an inch and he'll take a mile.

WHO'S WHO

WHO DOES GOD THINK WE ARE?

> God made the world
> and said, "That's *good.*"
> And when God made me
> he said, "That's *good.*"
> And I can *be* what God means,
> if I can *see* what God means.

Be ye perfect even as your father in Heaven is perfect.

—Matt. 5:48

See ye perfect even as your father in Heaven sees perfect.

Beloved, we are God's children now. It is not yet clear
what we shall be. We only know that when he shall
appear we shall be like him, for we shall see him as he is.
And all who have this hope in them, purify themselves
even as he is pure.

—1 John 3:2–3

And God saw everything that he had made, and behold,
it was very good.

—Gen. 1:31

SHOULD FIT

You never thought your baby was dirty even when you changed his diapers. Do you know he isn't a dirty rotten little brat even when he has a "should" fit? Do you know he is having your should fit and that he is doing his very best to have one as good as yours? Do you know that this is not anybody's fault—neither yours nor his? It is just a sign that something needs to be understood.

WHO DO YOU THINK YOU ARE?

When I'm mad
and he's bad
or she's sad
we're wrong.
God is
my me,
his he,
her she,
and our we.
Everything else
that seems to be
is only
phoney
baloney.

HOLY CHRISTMAS

Someday I hope the following story will be published as an individual picture book for children. There are so many beautifully illustrated editions of the Christmas story, but I have never seen one that could show a child what the story *means,* and what it has to do with one's own life. In my book the story will take place on the planet Earth—and in space—to show that it is not just about Jesus and Mary and Joseph in Jerusalem long ago, but about living and loving. And one thing that seems to get overlooked is that Jesus is the only person in recorded history whose parents thought he was a child of God rather than their own creative project and possession. This insight alone could revolutionize parenthood.

THE STAR CHILD

Yes, now it is time for bed.

Millions and millions of children are going to sleep. And millions and millions of stars are shining in the sky. Some say the stars are places where love shines through. Some say there is one star for every child and that each time a child is born there is another place where love shines through.

Once upon a time there were a man and a woman to whom was born a baby—a perfectly lovely child like you. This baby's mother and father knew for sure that he was a child of God—a gift from heaven, just like you. And so it happened that his star was very, very bright on the night that he was born. It was so bright I just can't tell you how bright it was!

Still, most people did not notice this bright, bright shining star. They had too much to do to be out looking at stars. They were too busy inside their lighted houses. And it is hard to see the stars when the lights are on, isn't it? Outside in the darkness on the hills were some shepherds. Often they built fires because they were afraid of the dark. But the fires they built were too small for the big darkness.

Otherwise there wasn't much to do out there on the night hills. So the shepherds were always looking up at the shining stars in the dark sky. Of course they saw the bright star of the new baby.

The only other people to see that star were three wise men. They had big houses with lots of lights and all the shiny treasures anyone could ever wish to have. Yet each of them still had one big wish. They wished to find something brighter and better than all the treasures on earth. The wise men saw the star because they were looking for light.

So the only people who saw the star of the baby were

some shepherds who had almost nothing and three wise men who had almost everything.

It was such an amazingly bright and beautiful star that the shepherds and wise men all got up and followed it. They walked and walked until finally they were standing right under the star's light. There they saw the star child with his star mother and star father. And suddenly they were filled with love.

Now they could see, too, that the baby was a child of God. And they saw that the light of the wonderful star was love.

In a little while the baby grew up to be as old as you. His name was Jesus. Jesus' mother and father explained to him that he was a child of God. Because he had been told that God was his father, Jesus naturally was very interested in learning about God. He learned everything he could about God from his parents and rabbis, and when he was older he made some important discoveries. He found out that God is love and that everyone is God's child. Jesus saw everyone in the light of God's love. No matter how unfriendly or sick or sad someone seemed to be, he could always see the star child shining through.

Not everyone understood what Jesus was talking about. But those who did lost all their fears, and their good wishes came true, and they were filled with love just like the shepherds and three wise men. Their stars grew very bright.

Because he showed so many people how to let the light of love into their lives, some have called Jesus the Light of the World.

Now let's put everything away and turn off the lights and be very still. Then we can look out the window to see if any bright stars are out tonight—one star for every child of God—one star for you!

BORN AGAIN

Until we know that we are children of God we think we are children of our parents and parents of our children. We are always trying to get our parents or our substitute parents to love and, therefore, support us. If we carry this too far we may misuse, even abuse others, including our children. It can be a kind of dirty business in which we wind up "shoulding" all over ourselves and each other. The result is that as we grow we may feel a bit dirty because of all our ulterior motives, harbored resentments, and secret rivalries. I think part of the appeal of the Christmas story and why we love babies in general so much is that we yearn to be pure and innocent and clean, good again—to have a fresh start and be truly lovable and loving.

So it's good to consider what the conditions were under which the Christ Child got born. Suppose the inn and the stable are really just two states of mind. What is the Inn Consciousness in which there is "no room" for the Christ Child? What is the inn too full of? People. Inn Consciousness is a headful of people trying to get ahead, looking out for themselves, by wheeling and dealing, prostituting, influencing, jockeying for position, and trying to get comfortable at each other's expense. It is very crowded and un-stable. Here there are only strategies, and it is no place for the Christ Child to be born.

What about the stable? In the stable are only lowly animals—beasts of burden. They don't think they know what's good for them. They don't have much and they aren't trying to get more. They don't worry about the future or where the next meal is coming from. They trust, serve, and are interested to see what's next. They are humble, open, and willing, like a baby. That's where the Christ Child gets born. All you have to do to maintain a stable is to keep shoveling out the manure and bringing in fresh food. To maintain Stable Consciousness all you have to do is keep shoveling out the "should," keep letting in fresh inspiration and be willing to do what is called for. That's where the Christ Child gets born. That's how our Christ-self can be born in us, fresh and clean as a baby, newborn, born anew.

Behold I make all things new.
—Rev. 21:5

DEAR WALTER

Dear Walter,

. . . Hope you had a fine Christmas. Ours was hectic but
wonderful. The children are at such a sweet age. Also they
are so confused about everything. This afternoon I
overheard three dress rehearsals for Jesus' birth. A fur hat
with a small doll secretly tucked inside was placed on a
stool. Andrew (1½) was then directed to sit on the fur hat
on the stool. He was supposed to be Mary riding to
Bethlehem on a pony. After being shoved across the floor
to a pile of blankets he had to get off the pony. Jan (3)
then took the fur hat and delivered the baby. "Surprise,
Andrew—it JESEZ! Now we have to put him in the manger
(the blankets) and then it's my turn to be Mary." Andy is
laughing all the time, just happy to be included. I am
laughing all the time, just helpless.

Hope you all are fine, too. Happy New Year.

Love,

Polly

Jan remembers that when it was his turn to be Mary the fur
hat with the doll hidden inside was held over his tummy. It was
a year and a half after the birth of his baby brother, and his
first really conscious Christmas. Clearly he felt both wonderful
surprises had something to do with each other and were worth
celebrating.

WHO DID THEY THINK HE WAS?

The fact that Jesus' parents did not *think* he was *their* child is really something to consider. Even before he was born they said that he was a child of God. I know of no other parents in history who have from the very outset regarded their offspring as God's and *not their own*. To my knowledge the possible effect of Jesus' parents' perception of him has never been examined. But I think it can be no coincidence that it was the child of such parents who so young said to his mother and father that he had not followed them home because he had to stay with the rabbis to "be about my father's business," and who so early in adulthood made the discovery that "I and my father are one." Everyone else has to be reborn, to discover a new parent, before the struggle to keep or win a parent's love can cease.

NOT TOO CAREFULLY TAUGHT

I was lucky enough to grow up free of racial and religious prejudice. Not that my parents weren't prejudiced. They were. In fact, it was partly due to their prejudice that I grew up without it. Throughout my childhood we moved from one exclusively white, Christian community to another. As they say, you've got to be carefully taught, and I wasn't. I simply didn't find out about racial prejudice until it was too late for me to acquire it. I did grow up playing cowboys and Indians (frequently preferring to be an Indian). I did learn about slavery in grade school, and that it was wrong. But I didn't become aware of current racial and religious prejudice until I was in junior high school. By then there was one other factor in place that made me impervious to any such indoctrination, and that was my own experience of not belonging. Thanks to many moves and certain family problems I was all too familiar with the experience of being a newcomer, of not fitting in. So when in seventh grade civics class I first learned of present-day racial strife, it came as a shock. I knew it was awful. When I brought it up at dinner that night and my own parents sheepishly admitted their prejudice—against blacks and against Jews—I was appalled. So I sailed smoothly into the sixties with my only prejudice being against prejudice.

Oddly enough my oldest child, growing up in a liberal and somewhat integrated town, became aware of racial prejudice much earlier. I remember the incident fondly because it showed how unnatural such prejudice is. For a while his best friend—his first girlfriend—was a little black girl named Andrea, the granddaughter of a well-known educator. The child's mother had to leave for work before the nursery school carpool we both belonged to picked up her daughter. So Andrea often waited with me by the back door of our apartment building. On rainy mornings she and my son would scamper through the basement hall and in and out of the laundry room. Through the open round glass door of the dryer they kissed each other, laughing, mushing their lips against the glass. Briefly, and for the first time, this three-year-old and four-year-old were in love.

I don't know what he heard. But somewhere, perhaps in nursery school—where he happened to have a wonderful and beloved teacher who happened to be white and who happened to be married to a man who was black—someone had put something into his head. I was standing in the kitchen when he brought it up. He was sitting on the little swing we had suspended from the archway at the end of the dining area.

"Mom?" he called.

"Yes?"

"Can whiteskins marry blackskins?"

"Yes, dear," I answered.

"Whew!" he sighed with relief.

I continued working in the kitchen. I was so touched by the purity and precision of his choice of words: white*skins*, black*skins*. He just couldn't refer to the whole person by color. So clear. So dear. But then it occurred to me that in order to be asking the question he had to have heard something. It didn't seem fair to pretend that there was no issue whatsoever. I stuck my head out of the kitchen.

"Did someone say something to make you think it wasn't all right?" I asked.

He didn't want to go into it.

"I just want to know if whiteskins can marry blackskins," he repeated.

"There are people who have thought that it is wrong. There are people who have said that people of some colors are not as good as people of other colors. But that was a mistake, and it is changing. When you grow up, you can marry whomever you like."

"Whew."

See what love the Father has given us, that we should be called children of God; and so we are. The reason why the world does not know us is that it did not know him. Beloved, we are God's children now; it does not yet appear what we shall be, but we know that when he appears we shall be like him, for we shall see him as he is. And all those who thus hope in him purify themselves, even as he is pure.

—1 John 3:1–3

Love never ends; as for prophecies, they will pass away; as for tongues, they will cease; as for knowledge, it will pass away. For our knowledge is imperfect and our prophecy is imperfect; but when the perfect comes, the imperfect will pass away. When I was a child, I spoke like a child, I thought like a child, I reasoned like a child; when I became an adult, I gave up childish ways. For now we see in a glass darkly, but then face to face. Now I know in part; then I shall understand fully, even as I have been fully understood. So faith, hope, love abide, these three; but the greatest of these is love.

—1 Cor. 13:8–13

WHAT'S WHAT

BEFORE YE ASK

Wouldn't it be helpful if we could all keep in mind that Jesus was a Jew? Then there could be all kinds of Christian Jews and Jewish Christians, but we could worship together. Then there wouldn't have to be half-empty churches and half-empty temples and there would be much less overhead, because we could seek and find together. I'm not talking about homogenizing everything. That would be a shame. The light strikes the ground differently in different places. But looking at your own tradition by the light of others' is very illuminating. Mostly what we strongly disagree about is what we are both wrong about. Instead of defending our answers we should be deepening our questions. The Bible says "Before ye ask, I answer." It's the asking we need to be concerned about. It is the questions that form truth into answers. Arriving at the right question is arriving at the answer.

This is especially true with young people. Traditions are wonderful and important, but to impose beliefs is not helpful. I have seen many adolescents lose their faith when they turned for help and found their childhood beliefs meaningless. So it is much better to help young people with their questions than to try to get them to commit to your answers. I had a wonderful opportunity to found and lead a youth group on this premise. It was sponsored by a church, but it was not doctrinal. Teenagers of all denominations and sects attended this group, which provided a wholesome, loving forum for them to practice being together and talk openly about their concerns. Religion was not often discussed, yet it was a deeply spiritual group. Out of this group came seven teens who asked to meet with me about religion. Most were non-or disillusioned churchgoers, a couple were non-Christian. But they were so committed! Late sleepers all, they appointed one member as designated waker upper. Each Sunday after church I found him making calls in the church office. For more than four years, long-legged, beautiful, mysterious as deer, they drifted in from the mist of sleep. Fresh and wet from showers, sleepy-eyed, eager, they poured out their pain and questions, surprised and relieved to see that religious ideas actually meant something and could help them in their daily lives. They loved to examine these ideas through the language of other cultures, literature, and religions. And they loved each other.

NO EXCEPTIONS

Dear Mrs. Berends,

I really wanted to give you a proper thank you. I want you to know how exciting it was, . . . knowing that this was maybe the only place I could hear these things. . . . I feel that this study group has strengthened my whole faith. . . . I'm starting to see how the Bible which I'd never really taken time to truly look at before can be so helpful and relevant in my life. . . . So thank you once again. The study group was very special to me. Not only was it very enjoyable having lunch all together, but I feel I have a new desire to look deeper and understand more. If I don't see you around have a wonderful summer.

Love,

L——

P.S. "Thou madest known unto me the ways of life; thou shalt make me full of gladness in thy presence"—Acts 2:28.

I can still see the light in her eyes when we talked about Jesus as someone who had brought deeper laws of being to light. I compared him to the first swimmer, pointing out that probably everyone who saw the first swimmer float believed she was exceptional and was defying physical laws. Perhaps she was called the Amazing Unsinkable Woman. We talked about how she might have said about buoyancy what Jesus said about God: "I am come not to destroy the law, but to fulfill it. The floating that I do, ye shall also do, and even greater feats shalt thou do, because I have demonstrated this oneness with buoyancy. I and this buoyancy are one. The floater can only float because the buoyancy floats her. I and this buoyancy are one."

"Mrs. Berends!" she said, her eyes dancing and her voice breaking with excitement, "Do you know what this means?"

AFLOAT AND AFRAID

When one of our children was three or four we went to visit a family that had a backyard pool. It was an aboveground pool, a tank with no shallow end. Lifejackets were provided for all half dozen or so children, none of whom yet knew how to swim. Soon they were all bobbing in the middle of the pool. All except for one of our children. He huddled by the side of the pool, shivering and trembling. Hand over hand he went around the edge, only occasionally letting go with both hands, only for a terrified instant. Afterward he cried.

"Why can they do it, and I can't?" he said.

"Oh, honey," I said. "It's only that you are afraid. Soon you won't be afraid anymore."

"Really!" he said. "You mean if I'm not afraid I can do what they can do?"

"Yes," I said. "They aren't doing anything. They are just letting the water hold them up."

I was amazed by how relieved and happy he seemed as we drove home. The next day we went to the local pool. As soon as we got there he marched into the water. He stood in the water for about five minutes and then threw himself in head-first.

How like him we are. Thrashing about terrified in life, fighting over this and that, comparing ourselves to others, feeling envious and inadequate and in danger of sinking, clinging to things and fearing to go forth. And all the time there is something that would hold us up and provide us and enable us. If we only knew. If we only let it.

How unlike him we are. If only we could be so receptive and open and trusting. If we could entrust ourselves to a higher power, then we could entrust our children. Then they, too, would be more trusting, more life reliant and buoyant.

UNHUGS

A child needs both to be hugged and unhugged. The hug lets her know she is valuable. The unhug lets her know that she is viable. If you're always shoving your children away they will cling to you for love. If you're always holding them close they will cling to you for fear. A spiritual perspective helps us become aware of an underlying life-supporting force and makes it easier to recognize when which is called for, hugs or unhugs. Our grown sons say that they never doubted that they were loved. But as the following episode illustrates, I know that they sometimes doubted their viability.

His mouth was a veritable Nadia Comaneci. He wrapped his mind around concepts, his tongue around words like a gymnast. But he wasn't great on his feet, and I was protective and fearful of his getting hurt. I tried to help him so he could be one of the guys and not feel left out. It didn't help him learn and only undermined his confidence. When he had his first bike and I tried to help him, he quickly came to the conclusion that he couldn't do it. He tried (sort of) for as long as I would run alongside the bike, holding it up, but whenever I let go he would lose heart and slip off to one side. Finally, he was in tears.

"I guess by now you believe that you can't do this?" I asked at last.

"Yes!" he said, tears spilling over. "Why can they do it, and I can't?" he said, just as years before he had spoken at the side of that backyard pool.

In the back of my head I had already begun to understand the meaning of the problem: Too Much Mother. No trust in a Higher Power. *Put the ducky back in the pond. Put the fishy back in the sea,* I said to myself.

I looked down at my son and a thought came to mind. "Do you really believe that of all the little boys and girls on the earth God picked you out to be the one who can't ride a bike?"

He looked back at me and there was a little flash of startled recognition in his eyes. I turned and went inside. And he went off and rode his bike.

May we be with the Force!

LOVE

CHILD: I *love* you, Mom!

MOTHER *(hugging child)*: I love you, too!

CHILD: Isn't love great?

MOTHER: It's the greatest. Do you know where we get it?

CHILD: From God.

MOTHER: Right! So in a way I'm your sister and Daddy is your brother, because we are all God's loved children.

CHILD: So God is the real father and mother! That's funny.

QUIET
SEEING

FINDING A FOOTING

Our children learned to think of God not so much as a person but as a source of love and intelligence. Prayer was "waiting for God to give you a good idea." A few times when they said I love you, we talked about God as the source of our love for each other. If someone had a problem, after a time of hugging and listening, but before talking it over sometimes we would sit for a minute to see "what God has to say." The idea was that "personal minds," theirs and ours, are not all we have to go on, that there is something reliable beyond self and other to which we can turn. It isn't as if we knew this and taught our children. Rather it was something we all needed and were learning together. In their teen years we had as many interfering-parent/defiant-teen struggles as any other family, but there were also wonderful intermissions and remissions. I attribute these to our long-standing practice of turning to God. In the early years, God was sort of a secondhand interest of theirs. They were interested because I was, and in a scientific way. But in adolescence they began to know the need.

Once when one boy had a problem he said, "Can I talk to you impersonally?" I said, "You mean, not as mother and son?" He said yes, so we made an appointment and talked about how to go about finding one's spiritual balance in a romantic relationship. He was in an all-consuming relationship at the time for which he was abandoning everything he needed to do. Two people seemed to be trying to live one life: hers. We had fought quite a bit about it so that you might have thought he couldn't come to me. But when he got sick of his own consequences and was feeling desperate, he was able to set aside our relationship and come to me as a counselor. I think the reason this possibility existed is because he had learned that there was a resource beyond us both to which I often turned as well. He knew he was in over his head and needed some higher power that was bigger than both of us. We could talk that time because it wasn't as if he as the not-knower was asking his mother the knower, but both of us turning to a higher resource.

I see that more and more when the going gets rough they take time to pray in that old listening way that they learned as children. So I know that they are poised and will be all right. I was not able to spare them my problems, but they know where to go when problems arise. The important thing is for children and parents to become aware of God as the parent rather than feeling that parents are God.

SIDE BY SIDE

In the conversation mentioned previously, we spoke of bicycle riding as a model for loving relationships.

"I see," he said. "You can ride your bike real close to somebody else's if your own bike is very balanced and if you keep it moving."

"Yes. You can't lean your bike on the other person's. You can't climb off your bike onto the other's bike. But as long as you keep your own bike moving along it is possible to be quite close. When you find someone to love it's tempting to quit living your own life and start using the other person as a substitute life support. This makes us cling to bad relationships, and wrecks good ones. Then you crash. You have to keep riding your own bike. You have to keep living your own life."

"Will that make the relationship last?"

"If it's good for the relationship to last this will allow it to. But if it isn't meant to last this will allow you to get free of it."

"But I don't want it to end."

"Of course you don't. But how do you know what's good for you? And do you really want what isn't good for you? Maybe God has a better idea. Maybe God would give you better life support than your girlfriend. We aren't meant to use each other for life support, only to share the lives we are living."

"How do I know that? How do I know there is a God? How do I know my life will be good?"

"You have to test it. Here's a little book which is full of Bible quotes and short comments. When you are feeling anxious and can't stop thinking about your girlfriend long enough to do your homework, open this little book and see what catches your eye. Read that, take a moment to consider it. See if there isn't some way that it applies to your life right now. If there is, notice the fact that the idea you needed came to you somehow. That way you can prove that you are being supported by something. That's God. Then obey that idea and see if it doesn't lift you out of your worried state and get your life rolling again."

"May I borrow this book?"

"You may have it."

In the next few days I found that little book open everywhere. If he had just left home it would be near the door. If he had just come down to dinner, it would be somewhere near the stairs. If he had just finished studying and had a snack it would be open on the kitchen table. And he had begun whistling again.

"Have you finished your homework?" I asked out of recent anxious habit.

"You don't have to worry, Mom. I'm using the book, and I'm doing what it says. It is helping."

In fits and starts we got through the year. When we both turned and listened and trusted and kept pedaling along, it was good. When we didn't, we fell over, collided, and got tangled up. But the main thing was that he saw firsthand—as if in a scientific experiment—the difference between God reliance and self/other reliance.

IS ANYTHING TOO HARD?

Actually he had some experience with that book when he was in second grade. I hadn't shown it to him, but he saw me use it, and the Bible, and other books—in quiet times, which he knew I needed. So what happened wasn't surprising—just nice.

"Okay, sweetheart. Good night!" I said. "See you in the morning."

"Night, Mom."

Five or ten minutes later he came out, looking desperate.

"Mom! I just remembered! Tomorrow is the storytelling contest. I have to tell a story in front of the whole school. I forgot to practice my story! It's going to be awful! What'll I do?"

I remember the urge I felt to panic and get mad at him because I didn't want him to have a bad experience—in which case, he would feel awful, be more fearful, and flop. Often I did that. I also considered blaming myself for not being on top of things, and playing Rescue Woman, keeping him up, and trying to help him rehearse—in which case he would be exhausted the next day and think he needed me to get through life and feel fearful and that he was a flop. Often I did that. Or I could try to figure out a way to get him out of it by keeping him home or writing excuses—in which case more of the same. Often I did that. But this time, for once, I was prayerful. I thought, wait a minute, what's the issue here? Storytelling. Learning. Sharing. Not impressing or winning. This child loves stories. He knows lots of stories because he loves stories. Storytelling is part of who he really is. He is not on his own in this, and he is not dependent on me either. If he is peaceful and assured he will either be inspired and all will be well—or he will learn a lesson and all will be well.

So, having put the fishy back in the sea, I had this to say:

"I'm sorry you forgot to practice. It's too late to do anything now. But don't worry. You're a good storyteller. I'm sure God will help you. No matter what happens, you'll be just fine.

He was calm, although not convinced. "Okay," he said. "And I will go over my story many, many times before morning."

Five minutes later I checked, and he was fast asleep.

In the morning he recited his story. He did not know it by heart, but he had the gist straight. As he left for school, he observed my little book of Bible quotations on the table and stopped to pick it up.

"I think I'll just see what God has to say," he said.

He opened the book and read aloud, " 'Am I not the God of all creation? Is anything too hard for me?' "

He put the book down and looked up with huge round eyes, slowly shaking his head in wonderment.

"That's just what I *needed!*" he exclaimed. "It's amazing! How did it happen? I mean I just opened the book and got what I needed!"

"What do you think it means?"

"It must mean that God is really real."

"Yes."

"Wow!"

If you look at people they will either look at you or away from you. But if you look at the sky, usually they will look to see what you are looking at.

More is caught than taught.

GRACE

When my mother was a little girl her father always said grace at the beginning of meals. When she was older one day her father said, "Now, Mary, you are a big girl. You lead us in grace today."

Awed and thrilled, my mother took a deep breath, folded her hands, bowed her head and said boldly something like: "Blmphsgifthrlsriflledgsmthrpflgnrsblskhfamen."

Immediately she was sent from the table.

After the meal my grandmother went to my mother's room. "Mary," she said. "Why on earth did you do such a disrespectful thing? How could you? Whatever possessed you?"

My mother had no idea what she had done wrong. All those years she had listened to her father pray, and he had done it so fast that she had never heard anything but nonsense. She had never had any idea that anything meaningful was being said.

Even when they know the words to certain prayers and passages, our children may not have a clue as to their meaning. I thought it was a good idea to teach our boys the Lord's Prayer when they were quite young, and to go through it frequently at bedtime. I did not try to explain the meaning at first. I only told them that it was a very important prayer from Jesus, which had everything in it you could possibly need to live by. I also told them that you could spend a lifetime trying to understand it. They learned that when you say such a prayer it is also helpful to stop and consider the meaning of each word and phrase. It is a good prayer for children and parents to pray together because it begins with the idea that God is the parent, which is by far the

most helpful idea that any parent or child could hope to come
to understand.

> Our Father which art in heaven,
> Hallowed be thy name.
> Thy kingdom come.
> Thy will be done on earth
> as it is in heaven.
> Give us this day our daily bread,
> and forgive us our trespasses
> as we forgive those
> who trespass against us.
> And lead us not into temptation
> but deliver us from evil.
> For thine is the kingdom
> and the power and the glory
> forever.
> Amen.

I didn't fight sexist language in the Bible. When I could use
God instead of He without awkwardness, I did so. I explained
that God is Mother as well as Father. I think they understood
Father as Parent, and saw that so-called male and so-called
female qualities were equally necessary sides of their own
divine nature. Neither of them grew up to be sexist and when,
feeling overly stuck with the housework, I accused them of
that, they said, "We're not sexists, Mom—we're Momists."

BED AND BOARD

CHILD: Is it "give us this day our daily *bed?*" or "give us this day our daily *breath?*"

PARENT: Both are fine. Jesus said, "Give us this day our daily *bread.*" He meant that God feeds his spiritual children with everything necessary to live—food, ideas, love. When you say *bed,* it means God gives us our peace and protection. When you say *breath,* it means God gives us life. All three are true. God is love and peace and life, and we are God's loving, peaceful, living children. You can say *bed* or *breath* or *bread.* Whatever you like.

CHILD: Right now I'm tired from such a busy day, so I think I'll say *bed.*

I heard of a mother who took her son to the pastor of their church.

"Pastor," she said, "would you please listen to Billy say the Lord's Prayer? He's got it all mixed up."

So the minister took the boy into his office and asked him to say the Lord's Prayer.

"Our Father which art in New Haven, how do you know my name?" the child began.

"Well," said the mother, when the two emerged from the pastor's study. "Did you straighten him out?"

"No," said the pastor. "I wouldn't change a word of the way he says the Lord's Prayer. His way shows that he understands two important things about God: first, that God is very near, second, that God knows him personally."

A friend of mine recalls that when they were children her brother used to say, "Ourfatherwhichartinheaven. How would that be for a name?" Actually, that's not too off base either.

BEDTIME PRAYER

PARENT: Good night! Shall we have a time for prayers now?

CHILD: Yes, but what shall we pray?

PARENT: We could say the Lord's Prayer and try to understand what it means. Or you could pray a prayer of your own.

CHILD: I'd like to say one of my own. *(Long pause.)* But, Mom, I don't have a prayer of my own!

PARENT: When we pray we are trying to let God speak to us—to let God give us a good idea. Maybe if you close your eyes and listen God can even give you a prayer.

CHILD: Oh, yeah! He will. *(Long pause with eyes closed.)* Okay. I'm ready now. God *did* give me a prayer.

PARENT: Good. Shall we pray together?

CHILD: Yes. Here is my prayer that God gave me. We love God's ideas, and love is his best idea. Amen.

PARENT: Amen!

AMEN

Amen
means ah so
and so be it
that's the truth
and I see it.

IN THE BEGINNING IS THE WORD

Even on the cross Jesus was still dealing with the concern about self in relation to others. Transcending it is a lifelong task for everyone. Prayer and meditation help with this task. For our family reading turned out to be an excellent preliminary exercise in the practice of prayer, a way to free ourselves from overemphasis on self in relation to other. In reading as in prayer there is a turning away from other people (and from thought of other people) to privately invite new input into consciousness. We found that a love of reading contributed to our children's self-esteem, peace of mind, freedom to be individual, love, and spiritual growth.

Our children learned to stand by holding onto boxes of books. They climbed on boxes of books, and made walls of boxes of thousands of books that had been shipped to me for a survey I was doing. We didn't *have* books, we *lived in* them. We had getting-up and before-dinner and waiting-for-Daddy stories as well as bedtime stories. "Hurry up and get ready for bed or you won't have time to read!" Even when all else failed, at that cry they would drop anything to jump into pajamas and scurry off to bed with piles of books to "read" to themselves until I came to read aloud. There were plenty of bad times but bedtimes were remarkably peaceful. Bed was associated with peace. Sometimes they voluntarily put themselves to bed—and book.

A common assumption is that the child with good self-esteem is one who thinks well of herself, which in turn depends on others having let her know that they think well of her. Children certainly develop poor self-esteem if others express a low opinion of them. But the converse that high self-esteem comes from being praised is flawed. Both praise and blame cause children to pay attention to themselves in relation to others. This in turn causes them to pay less attention to their learning, which in turn causes them to learn less and to do less well, which in turn reduces self-esteem.

Self-esteem is not a matter of thinking well of oneself but of forgetting oneself. It is inevitable for children to become self/other-conscious. But these days the emphasis on comparison and relationship to others—acceptance, approval, power, and influence—is overwhelming. Even preschool children are constantly pushed in relation to other children, in day care and playschool and karate and Suzuki and Gymboree and playdates. When they aren't with others they are watching others being with others in television sitcoms. There isn't anything wrong with classes or playdates. But too often the motivation is wrong. We want them to be accepted, to get ahead, to stack up, not to fall behind or to be left out—as if they didn't exist except in relation to other children.

Real self-esteem is not a matter of thinking well of oneself but of being what one really is. A child is above all a learning being. The child absorbed in a book is lost in his real work, much as a musician loses himself in the music. Self-esteem is a nonissue when such fulfillment is taking place. On the first day of nursery school several children cried, but even with his mother beside him one boy was so vociferously distraught that the teacher asked them to play in the hall. Discerning that the child was not so much afraid of leaving the mother as of being with the other children, she invited them to come fifteen minutes early the next day. The child entered the empty classroom calmly and eagerly accepted the teacher's offer to read to him. Fifteen minutes later they were still reading when the doors opened to the rest of the class. He did not look up when the other children poured in, or when his teacher excused herself to greet them, or when his mother said good-bye. He just kept looking at books. When he was finished he got up and played beside his classmates.

Reading brings a peace that comes with self-acceptance. We are so oriented toward knowing ourselves in relation to others that we cannot stand to be alone without music or TV or telephone. We pass on this anxious mind-set to our children. A child who can lose himself in a book is a child who can stand peace and quiet. The child who has learned to be alone with a book knows herself as somebody she can stand to be with.

Each child is a unique individual with unique talents and interests. Standardized comparisons encourage children to evaluate themselves in comparison to others. Ideas of super-kid and all-around bestness present an overwhelming threat to self-esteem, from which high, middle, and low acheivers suffer equally. Ignored is the fact that maturation is increasing individuation. Everybody learns to walk and to talk, but the more we develop the more individual we become. This is why many children are happier in high school than in elementary school. In high school there are more individual interest groups—not all the boys play sports at recess. But why wait? If individual interests are fed, the unique incomparable individual develops, and self-doubt gets lost in passion. The child who follows his nose, from self-chosen book to self-chosen book (or any quiet interest for that matter), is following God's beckoning. He will never just run with the pack or get lost in the crowd.

Like prayer, reading is also a way of changing course. The misbehaving child is not a bad child, but a child governed by a bad idea. The disturbing ideas that lead to misbehavior are nearly always about oneself in relation to others. Once such an idea has hold of a child it is like the driver of a car. Depending on the strength of the idea, if you try to control the behavior you may just be setting up a collision. If you ask the child to control her behavior, you may just be setting her up for failure. Neither car nor child can behave better until there is a better driver in the driver's seat. So how are you going to get a better idea in the driver's seat? Time out for books! This is another idea that proved itself in our book-ridden home. Like any other parent when the going got rough I sent my children to their room—but with stacks of books—not as punishment, but as release time. Time to be released from some notion about each other by letting in a better one. A pile of books nearly always did the trick. It helped us to fulfill Paul's suggestion, "Be ye not conformed to this world, but be ye transformed by the renewing of your mind, that ye may prove what is that good and acceptable will of God."

Most family struggles have something to do with people trying to impose their will on each other. Knowing that my children's troublesome ideas were hand-me-downs from me, I also found that these reorienting reading times made the biggest difference if I "took time" for spiritual prayer or study when they did.

It is a well-known fact that many children are addicted to television. As teenagers they will face even more dangerous temptations. Too much television watching, vandalism, substance addictions, and sexual promiscuity all have roots in the quest for self-esteem. But young people who know the joy of reading have known self-acceptance apart from the self/other context and have something better to do than vegetate in front of the TV, hang out endlessly, or seek refuge in substance abuse because of peer pressure or as an escape from feeling down on themselves. Books are no substitute for friends, but long years of treasured healthy, quiet reading times help protect against unhealthy social temptations. Young people with such background tire of time wasting and grow sick of self-destructive experimentation sooner, because they have something better to turn to instead. Readers value privacy and require quiet time that can protect them from going overboard to be one of the guys.

The child who is at home with his own individuality and can stand a little peace and quiet is also better able to get along with others. Children may not know about self-esteem, but they do know whether or not they are loved, lovable, and loving. In encouraging them to look to others for their self-esteem we make love difficult if not impossible because we are teaching them to relate to everyone in two very unloving ways. Those by whom they wish to be loved become prey, and everyone else a rival or adversary. If we try to float by using others for support (such as praise or acceptance) we wind up fighting for survival and end up double drowning. Only when we rely on the buoyancy of the water are we safe and happy together in the water—sharing the joy of floating. Reading is like floating in that we rely on a sea of ideas rather than other's opinions for life support.

Once there were two children, a jock and a nerd. The intellectual was very bad at sports. He was very happy in class and miserable at recess. His parents tried to help him do better at sports so he could feel better about himself, but the more they tried the worse he felt. The athlete was good at sports but not much of a student. He loved recess and hated class. His parents tried to make him a better student so that he would feel better about himself, but he just began to stutter. You could not imagine two more different young fellows. Yet mysteriously they became fast friends. The jock began to call the nerd and to invite himself over. They spent many happy hours together. The jock's parent was very happy that he had such an intellectual friend. The intellectual's parents thought maybe now their son would develop an interest in sports. But eventually they noticed that whenever the two boys were together it was very quiet in the house. They listened at the door of their child's bedroom, but there was no noise. After a few hours the boys would emerge and say good-bye, thanks for having me over, I had a great time. *What great time?* From the sound of things they had neither talked or nor played, yet each said the other was his best friend. It turned out that they had been reading. Stretched out on the floor, reading separately together they found relief from pressure to prove themselves in the eyes of others, a way of being in love.

Reading aloud together can also restore harmony between parent and child. Many parents of young children find that when love is least in evidence there is nothing so helpful as taking time to read aloud. This is a way of changing the subject from self in relation to other to something else and of being *with* instead of *at* each other.

Books are not the only way. Not all children take to books, especially if there is a should involved. Almost any passionate interest your child is moved to pursue on his own can provide the benefits I have described. But one way or another, it is good to provide and respect peaceful private times. Besides the fact that they saw their parents seeking, I believe that the two most important factors in our children's spiritual growth were this habit of peace and the awareness of some power beyond self and other.

Acquaint now thyself with God, and be at peace,
thereby shall good come unto thee.

—Job 22:21

For God is not the author of confusion, but of peace.

—Job 34:29

Thou wilt keep him in perfect peace, whose mind is
stayed on thee . . .

—Isa. 26:3

Be still, and know that I am God.

—Ps. 46:16

WHAT DIES
AND
WHAT DOESN'T

DEATH OF A PET

In God we live and move and have our being.

—Acts 17:28

Thank you, God,
for lending him to me.
Because of him I learned
a little more about loving,
a little more about taking care,
a little more about letting things be.
Thank you, God.
He is one of the nicest ways
that I have ever met you.
I really miss him.
But I'm looking
for some new sign of you.
Please help me find it.

Amen.

COMING AND GOING

I never saw her
before she came my way.
But that doesn't mean
that she wasn't.
I don't see her now
that she's passed away.
But that doesn't mean
that she isn't.

It seems so sad
to have her go.
But I am glad
that I can know
we are still together
where we always were—
safe and sound
in your loving care.

Jesus answered, ". . . I know whence I have come and
whither I am going. . . ."

—John 8:14

GOOD-BYE

Good-bye is very hard to say
if you think it means
he's gone away
and is no more.
But good-bye is easier
when you know it means
"God Be with You."
And it does.
And He is.

HELLO

One other thing about good-bye.
Because God is love—
one good-bye usually means
another hello.

God is still with you
even when someone you love goes away.
Hello? Hello? Do you know where?
Hello? Hello? Can you find God there?

OUTGROWING

Dear Lord,
yesterday I got too big
for my best old jeans.
They were worn out and didn't fit.
So we threw them out.
They were all used up.
Today my Mom bought new ones
with an extra pocket for my things.
The old ones had gotten too tight.
The new ones are just right.

Today my turtle died.
We buried his body and shell because
he wasn't living there any more.
Dear God,
was his old life too tight?
Is he wearing a new one
that fits just right?

CHILD: What happened to that goldfish? Is it dead?
PARENT: Yes. It died.
CHILD: Why did it die?.
PARENT: I don't know. Maybe it was finished living.

CHANGING SHAPE

Once there was an idea
in the mind of God.
That idea turned out to be my turtle.
It used to live in a hole in the ground.
It used to live in an egg.
It used to live at my house.
It used to live in my room.
It used to live in a glass bowl.
It used to live in a turtle shell.

The shape of him and where he lives
keeps changing and changing and changing.
But I guess he just keeps on and on
living and living and living
in the mind of God.

CHILD: God is *always* thinking things up—like my turtle,
like me. God never stops thinking, does he? So we'll
probably never stop being!

CEMETERY

The following conversations took place over a three-week period when our youngest son was only three years old. We drove by a huge cemetery every day on the way to nursery school. He had never seen anything like it. It was one of our better deep discussions because for once I didn't try to answer bigger questions than he was asking. In fact when he finally got to the big question—which, of course, was *Are they going to put me in the ground someday?*—the answer came to him directly. The Bible says, "Before ye ask, I answer." In gently leading our children we really only have to go from question to question. Sometimes you can help a child to formulate a question that you are sure she has, but it is not helpful to answer a bigger question than she is asking—especially when it comes to the really hard ones. It is also not helpful to tell children what you don't actually *know* yourself. You can say, "That's a good, hard question. One of the hardest. I don't know the answer. I don't think anyone really does. I can tell you some possible answers that people have thought of, but nobody knows for sure. What do you think?" I could tell my son had solved his problem to his satisfaction when, after the third exchange, he never mentioned it again.

Week One

CHILD: What is that? What is that place?
PARENT: It's called a cemetery. Or a graveyard.
CHILD: What are those things? Those stone things?
PARENT: They are markers.
CHILD: What do they mark?

PARENT: A cemetery is a place where bodies are buried after people die. The markers tell which body is where.

CHILD: You mean *people* are buried there?

PARENT: No. Just their leftover bodies that they aren't using anymore.

CHILD: Oh.

Week Two

CHILD: Why do people bury people's bodies?

PARENT: It's a tradition.

CHILD: How did it get started?

PARENT: People used to think that the person and the body were the same thing. So they tried to keep the body safe. That's why the Egyptians made mummies. They put the mummies in stone tombs. They put a person's favorite things—his pets or toys or jewelry—in the tomb too.

CHILD: That's silly. What would a dead body do with toys and pets?

PARENT: Well, to me it's a little silly. But that's because I don't think the person is the same thing as his body. I think it's like your old clothes. When you outgrow your clothes we give them away or throw them out. But that doesn't happen to you, just to your old clothes.

CHILD: Yeah. And then I get nice new ones!

Week Three

CHILD: Mom, your peepee is your body, right?

PARENT: Yes, your peepee is part of your body. So is your hair and your arms.

CHILD: Yeah, and my tummy and my bottom.

PARENT: What about your insides? Is that your body?

CHILD: Yeah. My guts.

PARENT: Is your thinking your body?

CHILD (*thinks a while, then gladly*): No. Your body is yours. Your thinking is you!

SANTA CLAUS

CHILD: Is Santa Claus real?
PARENT: Is love real?
CHILD: Of *course* it is!
PARENT: What color is it?
CHILD: Not any color. You can't *see* love.
PARENT: How does it sound? Loud or soft?
CHILD: That's silly. You can't *hear* love.
PARENT: How does it feel? Smooth or bumpy?
CHILD: Mommy! You can't *touch* love!
PARENT: But is it real?
CHILD: Of course it is!
PARENT: So is Santa Claus.
CHILD: Oh, I get it. Santa *is* real. But he might not be real exactly the way you *think* he is!

I always felt it was good to reinforce the children's experience that good things can come from out of the blue and not just from parents. It's a very good idea for parents to practice, too. We often use our children, trying to be good "off" them, giving to get rather than to show love. "You owe me. D'ya like it? Don'tcha love it? Don'tcha love me? Isn't it great? Aren't I great?" (Forgive us our trespassing, our indebting.) My mother sort of knew this, only there must have been something fishy there because I remember one year when it backfired. She had written "from Santa" on all the Christmas presents she gave us. At the end of the morning when we put together a list of people to whom we had to write thank you letters and for what, we found we had received something from each set of aunts and uncles and a whole pile of things from Santa Claus. We turned to our mother crestfallen and said, "But what did you give us?" Oops.

GOD'S CHILD

God means good.
God's good is a special secret.
You can't see it or taste it
or touch it or have it or smell it.
But you can see it and be it.
God's good is a special secret.
God's good is love and peace
and joy, and it is perfect.
It can never be taken away or spoiled.
God's good is a special secret.
And the you that seeks it and finds it
and knows it and shows it
is God's child.

THE HUMDRUM
IS THE HOLY

TODAY IS THE DAY

Today is the day that the Lord hath made. Let us be glad and rejoice in it.

—Ps. 118:24

CHILDREN: Bye, Mom, see you later.
PARENT: So long. Have a good day at school. And do you know what day it is?
CHILDREN: The day that the Lord hath made!
PARENT: And what are you going to do today?
CHILDREN: Be glad and rejoice in it!

That was another Bible verse the boys committed to memory at a young age. We had the above dialogue a few times as they were going out the door. You couldn't do it more than a few times without it becoming meaningless. But it helped them learn the passage and they found it wonderful to consider that it wasn't only Thursday, or a school day, or the day that we were going to buy shoes. Something more was going on beyond just what was happening on the surface.

BOREDOM

Sometimes when I have to practice—
Sometimes when I have to clean my room—
Sometimes when I have to do my homework—
It's so boring
that I can hardly do it.

But I know that when it's boring
there is something I'm ignoring.
Life is never a bore
when I know what I'm for.

One of the children asked if there was anything I really hated—with a passion—could hardly bring myself to do. What he hated and could hardly bring himself to do was make his bed. I asked if he liked to wipe his bottom. He said he never thought much about it. But you don't do it because it's fun? I asked. No, he said, laughing, of course not! So then we talked about reasons for doing things other than because they are fun or feel good. For example, it wouldn't be fun and it *would* feel bad if you didn't wipe your bottom. Over the years I have come to see that the very best way to get out of the doldrums is to see what needs to be done and do it. It's the only cure surer than going to the woods. This is really the secret of self-esteem and fulfillment. Each of us is *for* something that God has in mind.

And it is always possible to know what God has in mind for each of us at any given moment. Or you could say that each of us is part of the whole, and that the whole needs us to be whatever part of it we are all the time, and that it is possible to know what is required of us at any given moment. *Make your bed* is a possibility. If you learn to listen and obey such momentary ideas you discover that God is mindful of you at all times, and in the process your life, your individual purpose will be brought to fruition. This is a much surer way to establish a sense of well-being and worth than is trying to make other people love you. It is also the best way to establish a truly loving relationship with others. I tried to pass this on to my children. None of us has mastered it. It is something we are still learning.

> In thy presence is fullness of joy, and at thy right hand are pleasures for evermore.
>
> —Ps. 16:11

FETCHING AND CHOPPING

Long ago in Japan lived two Buddhist monks. All their lives they worked together doing nothing but fetching water and chopping wood. All day long, every day, day in and day out, for years and years and years, they did nothing but fetch water and chop wood. Fetch and chop. Fetch and chop.

CHILD: Ugh! How boring! Was that really all they did?

That's all they did. But amazingly enough they were never bored—not even for a minute. In fact, they were joyful and laughing and happy all the time. They were so happy and glad that people wondered. How could anybody be happy doing such boring, unimportant work?

CHILD: I don't know. How? Maybe they were just stupid.

Eventually people got curious. Even the mayor and the rich people grew curious. They were curious because even though they were very important people and had everything, they were not nearly so happy as those two monks seemed to be. They wanted to know this: Are those two guys crazy? or do they *know something?*

CHILD: A minute ago I thought they were crazy. Now I'm beginning to think they knew something. Did they? Did they have a secret?

Indeed they did. Those powerful, famous, rich people came to the shack where the two monks lived, and they stood and watched them work. There went the monks, back and forth, fetching and chopping, just as happy and joyful as they could be—fetching and chopping and laughing and singing. At last the visitors went up to them. They couldn't stand it any longer. "What is this?" they asked. "How can you be so happy doing this boring work? You have nothing. You don't even get paid. It isn't fun. And nobody cares about you. Why aren't you miserable? What is the secret of your happiness?"

"Ah," said the monks, laughing and grinning from ear to ear. "But isn't it marvelous? Isn't it wonderful to be fetching water and chopping wood?" Whistling and singing and laughing they turned and went on with their work.

CHILD: That makes me feel like laughing! What a funny
thing to say—that fetching water and chopping wood
is wonderful. What did they mean? I want to know.

PARENT: They never explained what they meant. All they
could do was show it. They showed that there is a
deeper, better kind of happiness than power or wealth
or fame or excitement. I think they had found that to
be useful and orderly and loving and simply alive is
happy and full. They couldn't explain that but they
showed it in this mysterious way. And you know what?
They never wrote a book and yet hundreds of years
later we are still reading about them and trying to
understand their secret. They never made a painting
and yet the way they lived was a work of art that is still
being appreciated. They were not doctors or teachers
or police and yet are still helping people to be
healthier, wiser, and happier. They lived happy, useful
lives. I think they lived God's ideas for them and
proved that this was a very happy way to live.

. . . AND RAKING

We went to close the cabin for winter. We waded up the long, steep drive now knee-deep in beautiful brown leaves. The boys played happily through the day while we squirreled about in the house making preparations for winter.

Late in the afternoon our youngest child came to the door.

"May I rake leaves?" he asked.

A big leaf rake was found. It was long and awkward in his six-year-old hands. He tried it out, testing it scientifically.

"I think this is the way to do it," he said. "More like sweeping than like raking." He was so pleased to discover the words *leaf sweeper* printed on the rake. It seemed that he was getting the idea all right.

An hour went by and he was still raking, systematically making a long, narrow path down the long, steep drive. Now, more than one hundred feet down the drive, he looked adorably small and solitary. I started to shout out, "Good job!" but noticing his peace and deep concentration, decided not to distract him. A little later he came to the door.

"I'm still raking," he said. "I'm going to rake the whole driveway!" His eyes were bright.

It was dark. Everyone else had come in long ago. At last he came, standing his rake beside the door and climbing onto the bench for supper. His food was already on his plate.

"You know what I've been doing all this time?" he asked, leaning against me.

"Raking?" I said. "Have you really been raking all this long time?"

"Nope," he said. "Mom, I've been fetching water and chopping wood. That's what I was really doing. It *is* wonderful!"

He smiled down at his plate and sighed a huge, satisfied sigh.

He still hates to make his bed. But he has had glimpses. We all have.

GOING FORTH
WITH JOY

NOW AND FOREVER

For you shall go out with joy and be led forth in peace.
The mountains before you shall break forth into singing,
and all the trees of the field shall clap their hands.

—Isa. 55:12

When I was twelve years old I found those verses from the
Bible somewhere. It was the first thing that really turned me
on to the Bible. I have always gone to nature to overcome
loneliness and interpersonal unhappiness. Besides often
being the new kid in town, for some reason I felt pretty much
on the fringe of my family, too. So I was always hungry for love
and acceptance—except when I was outdoors. I never felt
lonely in the woods because I never wanted anything from
them that they weren't already giving. I never felt unhappy in
the woods because I never imagined that they wanted me to
be anything that I wasn't or to give anything that I wasn't able
to give. I did not go to the woods to be seen, but to see. I went
as a beholder and in beholding was myself held to my true
being. This passage from the Bible described a joy I already
knew and suggested it could last forever. To this day I still go to
the woods to find peace. I am there now. I still love this verse. I
love the whole chapter it came from. Of course, it was one of
the first ones I gave the children.

> I part the out thrusting branches
> and come in beneath
> the blessed and the blessing trees.
> Though I am silent
> there is singing around me.
> Though I am dark

there is vision around me.
Though I am heavy
there is flight around me.

—Wendell Berry, "Woods"

ALL THINGS BRIGHT AND BEAUTIFUL

All things bright and beautiful, all creatures great and small,
All things wise and wonderful, the Lord God made them all.

Each little flower that opens, each little bird that sings,
He made their glowing colors, He made their tiny wings.

The purple headed mountain, the river running by,
The sunset, and the morning, that brightens up the sky.

The cold wind in the winter, the pleasant summer sun,
The ripe fruits in the garden, He made them every one.

He gave us eyes to see them, and lips that we might tell
How great is God Almighty, Who has made all things well.

All things bright and beautiful, all creatures great and small,
All things wise and wonderful, the Lord God made them all.
                                    —Cecil Frances Alexander, 1848

Children are so close to the ground, so surprised and fascinated by every new thing that they encounter. Therefore, to look at nature for its significance is a wonderful way to introduce them to a spiritual perspective and to discover the invisible force or what Albert Einstein recognized at three years old as the "deeply hidden." Playing with a compass, and watching it work, it suddenly struck him that "something deeply hidden had to be behind things." The main thing is to alert children to the idea that there is something underlying that can provide and guide us perfectly as needed, which means, as Jesus said, we do not have to "take thought" for our lives, willing and wishing and controlling things—

NOT EVEN A MOUSE

Accordingly, when we were at that cabin one of the children became possessed with the idea of having a brown mouse. "Oh, I just wish I could have a little brown mouse. It would be so cute. I would just love to have a cute little brown mouse." All he could think of was a little brown mouse.

Now even in our small apartment we had always had plenty of critters. When bedroom lights went out fish tank lights went on, and the children fell asleep watching fish living and moving and having their being harmoniously together. There was a tiny chameleon that had come on a truck full of tropical plants. He was so skittish, except when he slept. Then you could take him from his bonsai tree and he would sleep so deep and lie so light on your finger, so trusting, like a baby. You could feel him breathe and be amazed. We had crabs and snails and turtles and kittens and guinea pigs (not all at once, mind you, but in succession). Observing what little heads and minor brains they had we recognized that indeed there had to be something great behind things to make them be and work so intelligently.

But all was not sweetness and light. There were lots of bad surprises. Each African frog escaped from the fish tank never to be seen again, and the cat did not look as if she had swallowed the canary. Our rabbit's inner ear infection wrecked his sense of equilibrium and made him twist his head and flip over violently and repeatedly until we finally had him put to sleep.

And the maintenance! Turtles were great as long as you could see them. But we soon found out that they were really turd-les. Three days after cleaning the tank you couldn't see them for the murky water.

And the crimes that were committed! We killed more than one creature with love. If we hadn't killed the chameleon we would have had to go on feeding it disgustingly smelly mealy worms and locating chameleon-sitters when we went on trips. But we did kill it. Out of the rain forest, or wherever he came from, the chameleon had to be hosed down daily, misted with a fine spray of water. I used an old Windex bottle filled with water. One day I gave the kids the wrong old Windex bottle, the one I used to wash windows, filled with water and ammonia. That chameleon died a horrible death. The good that we would, we didn't, and the evil that we would not, we did.

We did love them all. We saw how wonderfully and fearfully and beautifully they were made. But in retrospect, perhaps the primary revelation we received was that providing a jungle or a rain forest or a field or a pond or forest environment was no mean trick. What we botched with all our might for one mere mouse or fish, God did effortlessly and magnificently for all living things. Heaven and earth tell of thy glory. All things bright and beautiful, all creatures great and small. Maybe God could manage our lives too if we'd quit trying to run them ourselves.

At any rate, the day the brown mouse idea came up I was just not up for another bag of litter for another little critter, not even a cute little brown mouse. Maybe I had lost confidence. Maybe I was just wising up.

There was a little shed down the drive where tools were kept. When I went to return the rakes to the shed I happened to hear a little squeaking sound near the window. There were shutters over the window, and it was very dark. So I went and got a flashlight, and tiptoed into the shed with the children. There was a whole family of little mice living in the space between the shutters and the glass—it was a little mouserarium! We sat in the shed and watched those mice for a long time. Because of the glass they couldn't hear or smell us, and so, completely oblivious to our presence, went right on about their lives. We saw the mother feed the incredibly tiny babies, studied their tiny baby feet pressed against the glass, watched the mother wash and nurse them, saw them settle down to sleep as one, watched them wake and nurse, and run about.

So it wasn't all up to me! Down to even the tiniest tail and whisker and curiosity God would provide for my sons—and a creature was stirring, even a mouse.

> Look at the birds of the air; they neither sow nor reap nor gather into barns, and yet your heavenly Father feeds them . . . Consider the lilies of the field, how they grow; they neither toil nor spin; yet I tell you, even Solomon in all his glory was not arrayed like one of these.
>
> —Matt. 6:26, 29

GEESE OVERHEAD

CHILD: How do they decide which goose is the boss?
PARENT: I don't know. Which goose do you think is the
boss?
CHILD: The one out in front, of course. That's the
leader—the one that leads the way.
PARENT: I think we should look it up.

So we did, and we found out some amazing things. There is
no lead goose. The geese take turns being out in front. The
front goose is not the boss. The front goose is the servant.
Whichever goose is first has to work hardest to cut through the
air. The lead goose cuts through the air and creates a draft for
the others. Each succeeding goose gets to ride in the draft of
the goose ahead. By flying in a vee every goose gets to fly in
some other goose's draft—except the goose in front who has
to cut through the air and wind. Every now and then they
switch.

CHILD: How do they know when to take turns? How do
they know the way?
PARENT: Some people say it's instinct.
CHILD: I think it's God.

> Geese appear high over us,
> pass, and the sky closes. Abandon,
> as in love or sleep, holds
> them to their ancient way: what we need
> is here. And we pray, not

for new earth or heaven, but to be
quiet in heart and in eye,
clear. What we need is here.

    —Wendell Berry, "Wild Geese"

WHO DID YOU SAY?

When we speak
words come out.
When God speaks
birds come out.
You are a word
that God spoke too
What do you think
God means by you?

AFTER YOU

Father and mother of us all,
when I am in doubt,
afraid, unsure,
about how to act
or what to do
or who's who—
I pick out a friend—
one of your other children,
Jesus, or Buddha or Daniel
or the Peacemaker.
After you, I say.
And before I go my way
I step aside
and watch my friends go first.
They smile because they know
everyone they meet is
a child of God.
They walk tall and straight and sure
because they know they are princes and princesses.
They are not afraid because they know you are with them.
They are very sure because
they know you will give them
whatever idea they need
whenever they need it.
After you, I say.
I let my friend
lead the way.

Child, thou art ever before me, and all that I have is thine.

—Luke 15:31

It is your father's good pleasure to give you the kingdom.

—Luke 12:32

THE GREEN AND GRACIOUS DRAGON

Once there was a green and gracious dragon. He lived everywhere all the time. He was gentle and kind and loving and jolly, and he had a very special job.

One part of his job was to give peace to parents so they would not worry when children played away from home. The other part of the green and gracious dragon's job was to watch over children wherever they went. The green and gracious dragon knew how to do both jobs at once.

He could change himself into all kinds of happy places. And he did. He became wide waving fields where children ran after butterflies and flew kites and watched the sky. He became wonderful climbing trees. He turned himself into rolling hills for climbing and hiding and looking out. He became great bushes that hung over secret places. And he often turned himself into a brook nook. What's a brook nook? It is a place where a brook bends. To do this it has to slow down. Where it slows down for a turn the brook is very deep. Just around the bend there is a deep slow private place that is wonderful for swimming. It has smooth pebbles on the bottom and little fish and whirligigs, and it is called a brook nook.

The green and gracious dragon changed himself into all these cool beautiful places where children loved to go. Then he would just lie there all quiet and gentle, watching over the children as they climbed on him. He gave them beauty and good ideas. And even though the children didn't recognize the green and gracious dragon, they loved him all the same. And he loved them and kept them safe.

Parents who knew of the green and gracious dragon never worried about their children. "Have a good time," they said to their children. And the children were free to go because the parents knew the green and gracious dragon would be watching over them.

Now the green and gracious dragon's name was joy. And he is really a part of God. And there will never come a time when he falls asleep or ceases to be.

I will lift mine eyes up unto the hills; from whence cometh my help.
My help cometh from the Lord, who hath made heaven and earth.
He will not suffer thy foot to be moved; he who keepeth thee shall not slumber.
Behold, he who keepeth Israel shall neither slumber nor sleep.
The Lord is thy keeper; the Lord is thy shade upon thy right hand.
The sun shall not smite thee by day, nor the moon by night.
The Lord shall preserve thee from all evil; he shall preserve thy soul.
The Lord shall preserve thy going out and thy coming in from this time forth and for evermore.

—Ps. 121

THE PATHMAKER

It is easy to see signs of higher intelligence in nature. We are not so used to recognizing it in our own lives. Therefore, we find it hard to trust and tend to become very willful about looking out for ourselves and trying to get what we think we need to want. In the process we often oppose ourselves to good that would otherwise happen if we let it and insist on bad that wouldn't have happened if we hadn't insisted on it. Therefore, it's wonderful to find signs of higher intelligence in our human affairs.

One of the first signs I saw as a child was in the way paths occurred. Whenever we moved I always felt we really lived in a place when some new path had been worn. It was a remarkable mystery.

There was a big field behind one new house. On the far side of that field we found a new friend. So for the first time there was a reason for three people to cross that field: the friend, my brother, and me. One of us would go, or she would come—after school, on weekends, once or twice, now and then. Suddenly one day I noticed a path had been worn that we all took. Without any plan or agreement we had each chosen—or been guided!—to cross through that wide open field of tall grass over exactly the same route. Was it simply the shortest distance between two points? No, the path curved this way and that. Were there obstacles we had to go around that determined our course—or muddy stretches or inclines that influenced us? Not that I was ever able to discover. And yet this narrow path was worn bare.

Trust in the Lord with all your heart and lean not unto thine own understanding. In all thy ways acknowledge him and he will direct thy paths.

—Prov. 3:5–6

GRANDMOTHER

Grandmother . . . Grandmother . . .
Night and dark stars
are a beating heart
and moon the eye
of the world.
Let night be gentle
and moonlight
see with tenderness.

Grandmother . . . Grandmother . . .
Stones are fire
made firm, and
rain blood for the earth.
Let stones be warm
and rain flow
richly to heal.

Oh our Grandmother!
give these children
night for their being,
moonlight for their seeing
stones for their standing,
rain for their peace.

—Sheila Moon, "Knee Deep in Thunder"

LOVE
THINE ENEMY

ANTHILL

Most of our friends were from our own grade. But the girl across the field was a friend we shared. Of the three of us I was the fringe member. She was older than I, and closer to me in age. But she was closer to my younger brother in heart. They were braver in trees—much more daring, kindred spirits. They often traversed the treetops without me, had other paths that I had not helped wear and was not privy to. I often spent long afternoons drawing alone while they were out adventuring.

I was happy one day when my brother invited me to come along on one of their paths. They were going to show me a high honeysuckle hammock they had found, where no one could see you and from which you could see to the sea.

As I followed them along the path I felt happy, but soon I noticed they were whispering. The farther we went the more the whispering and excited giggling grew.

"Come on, Poll," my brother called in a sort of pretend friendly way, "we're almost there."

Whisper. Giggle.

It didn't work. I wasn't blind. When we came to the place in the path where the giant anthill they had found stood two and a half feet high and about three feet wide, they parted to pass on either side of it. I, too, stepped to one side. It was only when one of them said, "Rats," and they stopped going and made up some excuse to turn back and try again, that I understood. The whole plan had been to get me to step in the anthill.

Well, I didn't. I didn't step in the anthill and get ants all over my pants and in my socks. I didn't get stung by a single ant. But I was stung all the same. And stunned. Why? I wondered over and over, why would someone want to make some-one step in an anthill? What was it that made them want me to do so? What was it about me? Why?

It wasn't for many years that I began to sort that one out and saw how a mother's overcloseness to her son became a fortress the son would want to defend—how it wasn't me, and it wasn't him, or her, but it. I saw why sometimes he must have hated me for sitting on him and dangling my braids in his face! I saw why I had felt like doing that, and how unspoken tensions of our parents were felt and fought by us. I remem-bered hilarious times when our parents were out, when we played with our jello and laughed until milk squirted through our noses. And I forgave and loved us all. I could not protect my children against the hurt of others, but I could give them what I had learned to help them deal with it when it came.

THE ENEMY

Day One

PARENT: How was kindergarten today?

CHILD: Great. Except for my enemy.

PARENT: Your enemy! What do you mean?

CHILD: There's a kid who stands in line behind me. And he always hits me.

PARENT: What did you do to him?

CHILD: Nothing. I don't know why he hits me. He just hits me.

Day Ten

CHILD: Mom, why does my enemy hit me?

PARENT: That's still happening?

CHILD: Yes. Every day, and it's making me mad.

PARENT: Did you ask him to stop?

CHILD: Yes. He just laughed. A little while later he hit me again.

PARENT: I'm so sorry! I wonder what he's hitting you for.

CHILD: Nothing. I never did anything to him.

PARENT: Does he hit other children?

CHILD: I don't think so. He's only *my* enemy.

PARENT: Well, you could hit him back. Or you could tell the teacher. Or we could pray.

CHILD: How?

PARENT: Let's try. We know you are God's child. We know he is God's child.

CHILD: He's not acting like it.

PARENT: That's for sure. But I wonder what his hitting is for. Let's get quiet and see if an idea comes.

CHILD: Okay.

PARENT *(after a while)*: Is it possible that Kenny just wants to get your attention? Maybe he likes you and wants to make contact. Maybe he isn't *hitting* you. Maybe he is knocking on your door. Maybe he wants you to be his friend.

CHILD: Why doesn't he just say so?

PARENT: Maybe he's shy or afraid. Maybe if you ask him to play with you, he'll stop hitting.

CHILD: I'll try. But if it doesn't work I think soon I'm going to hit him.

PARENT: I would understand that.

I heard nothing further about Kenny or hitting. But a week later my son asked if he could invite Kenny over.

PARENT: You mean your enemy?

CHILD: No, I mean my friend.

Turning to God does not mean turning off or sitting on feelings. Children need to know that feeling bad isn't being bad. They need to know that their feelings are legitimate, that you understand and are sorry. Turning to God also doesn't mean things will always work out, as they did in this situation. It's best to turn to God simply with the idea of seeing what can be learned. The best thing to be found is the presence of something whose "thoughts are higher than your thoughts" and whose "ways are higher than your ways."

> For my thoughts are not your thoughts, neither are your ways my ways, says the Lord. For as the heavens are higher than the earth, so are my ways higher than your ways and my thoughts higher than your thoughts.
>
> —Isa. 55:8–9

ALL THINGS

All things were made by God and without God was not anything made *that was made.*

—John 1:3

All real events are signs of God and besides God does not anything happen *that really happens.*

All real people are children of God and apart from God is not anyone *who really is.*

CHILD: You know, I think sometimes you have to see the child of God in people even when they don't see it themselves.

WHAT A LAUGH

Today a big kid came at me.
He looked as mean as he could be.
Know what? I cut his strength in half.
Know what I did? I made him laugh.

HALLOWEEN MASK

CHILD: Once on Halloween, when I was little, I saw some
   ghosts. I was so scared!
PARENT: Yes, I remember that.
CHILD: But now at Halloween I know that witches and
   ghosts and monsters are just kids with masks on.

TOAD

They said my toad was ugly,
But I guess they aren't so wise.
They only saw his bumpy skin.
They missed his golden eyes.

Sometimes someone seems ugly
and mean and nasty, too.
Lord, help me then to see the good,
the golden truth that's you.

THE ONLY I AM IN THE WORLD

Then Moses said to God, "If I come to the people of Israel and say to them, 'The God of your fathers has sent me,' and they ask me, 'What is his name?' what shall I say to them?"

God said to Moses, "I am that I am." And he said, "Say this to the people of Israel. 'I AM has sent me to you.'"

—Exod. 3:13–14

THE PEACEMAKER

There was a school in Japan, a school for monks. Young boys were sent there to learn to live in a holy way. But for a time there was trouble in the school—lots of fighting and foolishness and disorder. The teachers in the school tried, but they could not control the situation. Finally the head of the school wrote to the head of all the schools.

Dear Master,

I think I have found the source of all the trouble. We have three boys who are troublemakers. They will not stop making trouble. Punishing them does not work. They will not stop making trouble. I am writing to suggest that we throw them out of school. Once these troublemakers are gone there will be peace.

But the master of all the schoolmasters wrote back quickly.

Please don't do anything. I'll be right over.

In a few days the master of masters arrived. He was a Peacemaker, too. In fact, all through the country people had noticed that wherever he went it seemed as if a festival were going on. He was so loving and jolly and kind and peaceful that wherever he went people just started to be happy.

So this Peacemaker came to the school with his suitcase. And do you know what he did to those troublemakers? Not anything! Except that once a day he required the three boys to meditate in his presence while he meditated. Otherwise he just lived there in his loving, peaceful, jolly way. Within a week there was no trouble at the school anymore. No more trouble and no more troublemakers. He didn't have to get rid of those boys or punish them in any way. In the presence of the Peacemaker everything was beautiful.

CHILD: Did that really happen?

PARENT: I read that it did.

CHILD: Could I be the Peacemaker?

PARENT: Of course. Jesus said, "Blessed are the peacemakers for they shall be called the children of God." Now let's close our eyes and try to see the face of the Peacemaker. How would he look? Can you see the Peacemaker? Can you see his eyes? Or her eyes? How would he look? How would she look? How would you look? Can you see the Peacemaker's face? Is it friendly and loving? Are his eyes kind? Can you see the Peacemaker?

CHILD *(laughing)*: I can! And my face is laughing. My face has light all around it! And—and—Christmas is coming!

PARENT: Good night, Peacemaker.

TOUGH MOMENTS

IT'S NOT EASY BEING GREEN

There were two other pairs of children in our apartment building. Sebastian (the oldest) and Samantha (same age as Jan), and Amy (same age as Jan and Samantha) and Ivan (same age as Andy). All six children played together, but Amy and Samantha were best friends, as were Andy and Ivan. Amy and Ivan moved away to the shore, and one day their parents said they could each invite one old friend for the weekend. Amy invited Samantha. Ivan invited Andy.

Day One

CHILD: Mom, why did they only invite my brother for the weekend? Why not me, too?

PARENT: Their son is the same age as your brother. You are older. Do you have other friends?

CHILD: Yes, but they have a boat, and they're going to swim and catch crabs and sleep out! It makes me so mad!

PARENT: Maybe there will be something just as good for you to do.

CHILD: But I don't want to do something else. I want to do that. I feel so angry!

PARENT: Yes, I understand. I know it's hard. But the feeling will pass.

Day Two

CHILD: Mom, I still can't stop thinking about the weekend. I just *wish* that I could go. I still feel so mad.

PARENT: Would you like to know what that feeling is? Would you like to know its name?

CHILD: What is it?

PARENT: Envy. It's a feeling of thinking that someone else has something good and you don't. You want what someone else has.

CHILD: Yes. I wish I could go, too.

PARENT: Well, you know you can't. But if you can get over the envying thought the bad feeling will go, too. Would you like that?

CHILD: No. I just want to be invited, too.

PARENT: I understand. Just so you know that there is a way for the feeling to go when you are tired of it.

Day Three

CHILD: Mom. I still have envy. I want the envy to go away. I want to go on the weekend. If I can go on the weekend the envy will go away.

PARENT: You can't go on the weekend. But there is a way for the envy to go away—if you are willing.

CHILD: Okay. I'll try it. I don't want this feeling anymore.

PARENT: You need to know that God's good is for everybody. In the Bible it says, "It is God's good pleasure to give you the kingdom." God will have a good idea for your weekend just as he has a good idea for your brother. If you can stop thinking about God's good idea for your brother and wanting it for yourself, maybe you'll have a chance to notice his good idea for you.

CHILD: How? I still wish I could go.

PARENT: Think about this. "It is God's good pleasure to give you the kingdom."

CHILD: It's hard. I still keep thinking about the weekend.

PARENT: I will help you. Let's pray together. (*We bow our heads and close our eyes. I don't remember whether we held hands this time or not.*) Dear God, I know that you love everybody. I know you have good ideas for each of us. I know you have a good, happy, wonderful idea for me—as good as your idea for my brother. It may be a different idea, but it is just as good. It is your pleasure to give me the kingdom. You love me, I know. I will just go on now—just doing whatever is next. And I will wait and see. I'll be looking and I'll see your good ideas for me.

CHILD: Mom! It's okay now. The feeling is gone. Finally! It's really gone. I don't have to have it any more.

PARENT: Wonderful! Now shall we do the grocery shopping?

CHILD: Okay. And how about if we buy some stuff to make cookies?

A year after I had written this down I showed it to my son.

"Mom, that's not how it ended!" he said.

"No? How then?"

"After we made cookies I went outside. I met Sebastian and his grandmother, and they invited me to go to see *Godzilla versus the Cosmic Monster.* Don't you remember?"

"Yes, now I do. Wasn't that wonderful? What do you suppose the cosmic monster is?"

"Well, in the movie he was big and green and huge."

"But I mean what do you think the big green cosmic monster stands for?"

"Oh, I get it. I guess the real cosmic monster is *Envy!*"

TWENTY-THIRD PSALM

The Lord is my shepherd,
I shall not want.
He maketh me to lie down
in green pastures.
He leadeth me beside the still waters;
he restoreth my soul.
He leadeth me in paths of righteousness
for his name's sake.
Yea, though I walk through
the valley of the shadow of death,
I will fear no evil;
for thou art with me.
Thy rod and thy staff,
they comfort me.
Thou preparest a table before me
in the presence of mine enemies;
thou anointest my head with oil;
my cup runneth over.
Surely goodness and mercy
shall follow me all the days of my life,
and I shall dwell in the house
of the Lord forever.

—Ps. 23

Besides the Lord's Prayer, I think this was the only other lengthy Biblical passage I helped the boys to memorize when they were young. As with the Lord's Prayer, we used it as a basis for prayer, reciting it out loud, separately or together, and then quietly considering its meaning. Think about what each word means, I suggested, and then see what it has to do with anything that you have been thinking about. I don't mean to say that they went on doing this with any regularity, only that they learned how to do it. It's a possibility that they know is there whenever they feel the need.

PARENT AND CHILD *(together):* The Lord is my shepherd. I shall not want.

CHILD: Is it wrong to want?

PARENT: No. Everybody does. But it hurts, and it isn't really necessary. I guess we could say, "The Lord is my shepherd. I *need* not want."

ANGRY

Dear Mom and Dad,
Please remember,
when I'm mad
I'm not bad,
I'm hurting.
Stop me
from doing bad things,
but don't call me
a bad person.

Then, please,
don't scold me.
Hold me,
or let me be
until I'm ready
for hugging and talking.
Don't ask me why
I did what I did
but what I felt
and how it felt
and when it began
and what would help.

Stand beside
not over me.
Stay with me.
Pray with me
until we see
what our real need is.

CHILD: I'm sad. I'm just sad. And don't give me any of your
hugs, because Daddy already tried that and it didn't work.
Right now I just need to be in a bad mood.

Dear God,

Sometimes I feel angry.
Everybody does.
It isn't so terrible.
But it doesn't work
and it isn't a happy way to feel.
Sometimes I just can't help it.
But after a while I get tired of
feeling unhappy and I want to be
happy again.
I can't help feeling angry sometimes.
But you can help me
when I'm ready.

So here I come.
I'm ready now, God.
Ready to be happy again.
Ready to give up the anger.
Ready to stop trying to have things my way.
Ready to start seeing things your way.
To do that here is how I pray:
God is love, so I am loving.
God is peace, so I am peaceful.
God is good.
Now I am getting going again.
I don't yet know what you have in mind.
But whatever it is,
I know it's fine.

HARD THINGS

From the bottom
a mountain is
a great big
hard thing
in my way.

From the top
a mountain is
a high place
where I can look
up and down
and far.

LEAVE ODD THINGS
WHERE YOU FIND THEM

As it turned out there was some sort of a reason why swimming and bicycle riding and other things requiring physical coordination didn't come easily to one of the boys. As I watched them grow I saw that one could throw a ball quite naturally with no practice whereas the other one could work and work at it and it still came out crooked and futile.

When they began to read and write, the difference became even clearer. Both loved books and learned to read early. I observed that the one who had barely learned to read and write could spell words he didn't even know the meaning of. From the get go his handwriting was clear and ordered and legible. The handwriting of the other one came out looking like bird poop no matter how hard he tried, and he misspelled and misread words he could use and define perfectly. Math papers showed right numerals but wrong answers to simple arithmetic. "What's the answer?" I would ask. "Thirty-two!" he said. "See? Thirty-two!" But the answer he had written and to which he was pointing was twenty-three. When he got higher in grade school his papers often came home with the remark "Messy. Sloppy. Careless." He wrote shorter and shorter papers.

Eventually I took him to an eye doctor who gave him a rolled up piece of paper and told him to use it as a telescope. He took the paper from the doctor with his right hand and held it up to his left eye.

"See that?" said the doctor. "Cross-dominance."

A neurological explanation! I do not know whether this was psychological or neurological in origin, but there it was regardless, to be dealt with one way or another.

You do what you have to do, I always say to myself, while seeking to know what you need to know. In taking him for the eye test I had done my doing and now prayerfully beheld him as perfect, capable, whole, and free. Otherwise I did nothing much about the problem other than explain it to him and a few of his teachers.

"Spelling is hard for you, but it is not because you are stupid. Writing neatly is hard for you, but it is not because you are sloppy or lazy," I said. "Many things are easier for you than for other people, but this thing is harder. Everybody has something hard. This is your hard thing. But you still have to do it."

So he had to accept that once he had written a paper he would have to copy it over before someone else could read it. We did not seek remediation because we felt his own high motivation would get him through, whereas remedial classes and exercises might only bore him and give him an excuse. No fool, he, he continued to write the shortest possible papers for a while. But when he reached high school we got a computer, and he began to write at length. If the problem had been worse, if he hadn't tested off the wall on standardized tests, if he hadn't already learned to read, we might have done more, but we would have still explained it to him as we did. It wasn't a flaw; it was a challenge. For a while he went on reading and writing crookedly, letters and numbers. But he's the one whose verbal and conceptual ability was like Nadia Comaneci's gymnastic ability, and he surprised and delighted his professors by the way he always came at things from left field.

Sure we have to be concerned with minimum competency, but not with all-around superiority. And you can't tell what a child needs by comparing him to others. Every individual is unique. Some plants grow deep roots before they break the surface. Some plants bloom once a year. There are as many ways of being as there are beings. You can try to see and to meet needs. You can try to maintain ideal conditions. You can do what you have to do, while seeking to know what you need to know. But what you need to know is to let them be.

When he was only five this same child tried to write a musical. He was so enthusiastic that from simply being shown how to place his hands on the keyboard and advised to use all fingers he taught himself to touch type. One of the songs he wrote and typed was called "Leave Odd Things Where You Find Them."

THE GOD OF
ALL CREATIVITY

PEN AND WHISTLE

CHILD: Isn't it wonderful? You might not have any idea of what you're going to write. But when you sit down with a paper and pencil and start writing, it just comes!

CHILD: Isn't it amazing how you can whistle? You just have this tune in mind, and when you whistle it comes out that tune! How does that happen?
PARENT: I don't know.
CHILD: I think it's God.

The Father worketh hitherto, and I work.

—John 5:17

A GOOD IDEA

CHILD: I want to draw a Christmas tree, but I don't know how. I can't do it. Will you show me?

PARENT: No. First, why don't you start by getting a piece of paper and a pencil? Then sit down quietly for a minute and wait. Maybe God will give you a good idea.

CHILD: Oh, yeah! I forgot!

(He runs for the materials then sits on the sofa—eyes closed, pad in lap, pencil in hand resting on paper, feet sticking straight out.)

CHILD: Mom! Look!

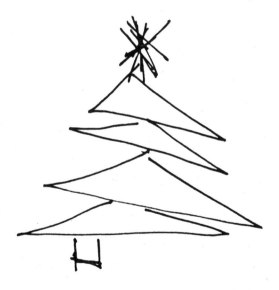

HOW TO GET GIFTS FROM
AN ELEPHANT

I had a nice time visiting a school and talking to children about being an author. The children had already read *The Case of the Elevator Duck,* and the day I came they were shown the movie. Afterward we met together. As usual the first question they asked was, "Where do you get your ideas?"

"Where do ideas come from?" I asked.

"Your mind . . . your brain . . . your imagination," they offered.

"How many of you think writers and artists have better minds than other people?" I asked.

As usual a disappointingly large number of hands went up.

"So does the mind make ideas?"

"Yes."

"Really?"

"No?"

"Then how do we get ideas?" I asked. "How does a radio play music? Did you ever look inside a radio?"

"Yes."

"Did you see any music? *(Laughter.)* Any tiny violins? Any itty bitty singers? *(Ha ha.)* So how does the radio get the music?"

Eventually they got it together that the music is broadcast by a radio station and travels through the air to the radio. We talked about how the room we were in was already full of all the music and baseball games and advertisements being broadcast in the area.

"So what is necessary for the radio to play music?" I asked. And in a few minutes they had come up with the answers.

"It has to be plugged in!" said one.

"Turned on!" "Tuned in," offered others.

"So do we," I said.

Now I asked how many of them were good artists. The numbers go down as the grades go up. In a kindergarten class nearly all the children would have raised their hands. In this fourth-grade group of about sixty children, five hands were raised. Isn't that tragic?

I told them about my son's Christmas tree drawing, pointing out that then he was three and short and by now he was over six feet tall, and that in the meantime he had become quite a good artist whose pictures had won prizes and been hung in the state capital.

"How do you think he learned so much?" I asked.

"He was plugged in, turned on, and tuned in," they shouted.

Next we tried it together. I said I would show them how to get an elephant to give them some presents and asked how many knew how to draw an elephant. Two hands went up.

"So if I asked those who can draw an elephant to do so, only two of you would try?" I exclaimed. "The rest of you would just sit there and wait? Isn't that a pity? But today we will draw an elephant together."

I drew what they told me to draw on the blackboard. We started with what we knew: trunk, tail, etc. In the process we found out lots of things that we didn't know: how the head is attached, where the ears are located. The result could not have been mistaken for a rabbit. But some parts looked funny.

"Now the next elephant you see is going to give each of you six or so presents! Right?" I said.

"I get it," said one child. "We'll get the answers to the questions we got from drawing the elephant. Get it?"

They got it.

Dear Mrs Barens,

Thank you for coming to our school. I liked how you were so calm. We play squiggle every day. Now I know I can draw. I made a story about my squiggles. But now my big problem is I don't know if I should be a writer or a illustrater. One more thing I have to tell you is you remind me of my mother.

Your friend,

Amy R—

What we were really working on that day was prayer. You can't talk about prayer in school, but in fact that is what the children were learning. Writing and art are not forms of self-expression, but of divine expression. Prayer is the way that ideas get into us so that they can use us to express themselves. If we don't try we don't find out what we don't know. If we don't find out what we don't know we can't learn. If we don't receive we have nothing to transmit.

At the end of my visit I taught the children a drawing game called "squiggle." I made a squiggle on the blackboard, and invited someone to come up and make a picture out of it. Eventually I copied one squiggle three or four times and had three or four children complete the same squiggle. The result was three or four completely different pictures.

"That's the difference between a radio and you," I said. "Any radio tuned in to the same station will play the same music. But when you are plugged in, turned on, and tuned in *different* beautiful things will come through each of you. You are completely unique. So if you don't let life's music play itself through you it's never going to be played.

So far, unfortunately, you can't talk much about religion in the classroom. But the process we are talking about is an exercise in prayer all the same. Because God is where ideas come from, and they do come, if we are plugged in, turned on, and tuned in.

CHRISTMAS ELF

PARENT: Remember that Christmas tree you drew? How about drawing one that we can use for our family Christmas tree this year?

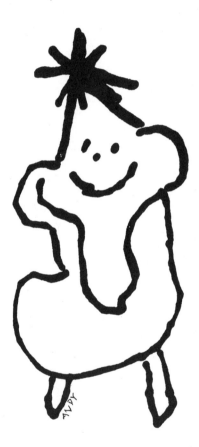

CHILD: Okay. I'll do it right now.

CHILD: Look! I started to draw a Christmas tree, but God gave me a different idea. Would this be okay?

PARENT: Oh, yes, it's wonderful. A Christmas elf!

DIVINE MATHEMATICS

Children can learn to look for and prove to themselves that God exists and is present in their lives. Begin with a need they can recognize. Children often experience the need for guidance, so they are interested in God as a source of guidance. They are eager to hear that they can listen for and receive guidance firsthand—without parents as intermediaries. They will pay attention when you explain that. And then they will go out and try it. I suggested the following to some fourth-grade Sunday-school children:

"Next time you feel afraid and don't know what to do, remember God. Before you worry any more and before you ask your parents or your teacher for help, become still and remember that God can help you. No matter what's bothering you, for just a minute be as calm as you can and listen. See if an idea comes. If an idea comes that you didn't have before, you will know that God has spoken to you. And next week come back and tell us what happened."

In the next class I asked if anyone had tried it.

"I did," said one child. "There was a substitute teacher in school and I had been out sick. They were going around the room and everybody had to do a math problem. But I didn't know how to do it. I felt more and more afraid. I tried to be calm. I thought about God like you said, but I still didn't know how to do the problems. But when my turn came the teacher skipped me and went on to the next person! Somehow she knew! After class she showed me how to do it. Was that God? I think that when I prayed, God gave *her* an idea!

OKRA

My friend Florence Nightingale Mitchell grew up in the South, graduated from Tuskeegee University when she was seventeen, and had been shot at more than once for being black. She was second to Babe Didrikson Zaharias in the Olympics in the shotput and the javelin. She was six foot four inches, had the biggest feet I had ever seen and the best laugh I had ever heard. When we first became friends I was eighteen and uncertain about a lot of things, she was forty and going through a divorce. We helped each other through some rough times. Flo insisted that we tell each other our life stories. One story she told was how she found out for sure that there was a God. She was eight years old, visiting an old crosspatch aunt of whom she was terrified.

"I'm going out, Florence," her aunt said one afternoon. "Before I get back be sure you fix that okra. Hear?"

"Yes, Ma'am," said Flo to the door, which had already slammed shut behind her aunt.

Fear welled up such as she had never known before. "Oh, Lord! Now what am I going to do," she thought, feeling the strange-looking vegetables. "I don't know how to fix okra! Aunt's going to kill me when she comes back!"

So she got down on her knees before the kitchen table with the okra on top, and prayed, "Dear God, *please* help me fix this okra! You've just got to help me fix this okra, or Aunt's going to kill me! Please help me fix this okra!"

After a while she got up and went to work on the okra, and when the aunt came home Flo waited, her heart pounding.

"My, now, that's fine, Florence," her aunt said. "You fixed that okra just fine."

That's when Florence Nightingale Mitchell knew there was a God.

WORSHIP

TOO SAD

Like Bible reading, church is another thing that never quite fell into place. For years I wasn't comfortable in church. The emphasis and the reliance on Jesus himself didn't seem true to me. I thought Jesus would hate it. When the children came along I wasn't sure what to do. I felt the teachings of organized religion were misleading and couldn't see how they would be helpful. At the same time I was very eager for them to be educated in the Bible and to become spiritually conscious. I didn't feel it was desirable for us as parents to be their only teachers, but I couldn't find a church that I thought would really guide them.

For a while they went to a Christian Science Sunday school. I did not care for the exclusive emphasis on Mary Baker Eddy either. I had reservations about the absolute avoidance of medical measures. Otherwise, although stated in rather old-fashioned language, the teachings seemed truly spiritual and valid. They spoke of getting beyond personal mind, saw the answer to problems in terms of spiritual awakening and clearer seeing, looked at Bible stories for meaning relative to everyday life, and emphasized prayer and meditation as essential to living.

Because what the children had been learning at home was similar, the boys were fascinated and enthusiastic. They appreciated what they learned and felt good about themselves in class. Their contributions to discussion, similar but formulated differently, seemed to their Mary Baker Eddy—reliant teachers "spiritually brilliant." All in all it was happy and worthwhile.

Because as a nonmember I was not invited into Sunday school, afterward on the way home I tried very hard to find out what had gone on. When asked how Sunday school was, the usual response from one boy was, "Perfect!" Until one week.

"How was Sunday school?"

"Perfect," he said automatically, then, "No, something sad happened."

"What?"

"I don't want to talk about it."

"Tell me, please. I want to know."

"Well—no, I can't. It's too sad."

When pumping got no result, I began guessing.

"Did something happen? Was Jerry (who appeared to have some sort of emotional problem) upset?"

"No."

"Did someone seem (speaking good Christian Science) to have died?"

"Yes."

"Who?"

"The head of the Sunday School."

"What? Mrs. Templeton! Are you sure?"

"You know that lady with white hair who laughs all the time—that's who. The head of the Sunday school. I thought her name was Mary Baker Eddy."

It took a while to put it all together. Much reference is made in Christian Science to "Our leader the Discoverer and Founder of Christian Science Mary Baker Eddy." From this the children had always assumed that their leader the head of the Sunday school, whose name they didn't actually know, was herself Mary Baker Eddy. When Mrs. Templeton, who was on vacation, hadn't appeared, they had asked their teacher "Where is Mary Baker Eddy?" and been told that she had passed away. It was too sad. It was funny. But it was sad. I think Christianity has tended to make a similar sad mistake.

TEACHER: When we speak of Jesus, we usually call him Jesus Christ. What do you think "Christ" means?

CHILD: Well, "Jesus" was his name. That's *who* he was.

TEACHER: Right.

CHILD: "Christ" must be a way of saying *what* he was.

TEACHER: Very good!

CHILD: I think "Christ" means God's best idea of human.

TEACHER: Wonderful!

GOING TO SEARCH

We stayed with that Sunday school for a year and a half, and then went back to muddling along on our own. After we had logged in a few more miles and a big threat settled over our household that made it clearly important to expand the boys' spiritual community to a larger circle of adults. By this time we had moved to a very neighborly street. Besides the owners from whom we had purchased our house and who claimed to have "willed" us to their local church as part of our contract to buy the house, there were three lovely welcoming families nearby who belonged to the same church. We just went with the flow and joined, too.

Had I understood either less or more we might have gone to church sooner. There is no right or perfect church to be found. Church is for the search. Wouldn't it be better if we said we were going to search? When you understand third-grade math you don't belong in third-grade math classes. If we understood what parenthood has to teach us we wouldn't belong in parenthood. If we understood how to be perfect spouses we probably wouldn't belong in marriage. According to the Gospel of Thomas, Jesus envisioned such a day, "when they shall neither marry nor be given in marriage." If we understood our oneness with God we probably wouldn't need churches or temples or mosques. Jeremiah envisioned such a day, "when no one shall teach his neighbor saying, 'know ye the lord,' for they shall all know me, from the least of them to the greatest." Meanwhile, thank goodness for the learning.

A DIEU

MARTIN

A huge, hard event that took place in my son's childhood was the death of the father of one of their friends. It's not only that we were friends as individuals. Our whole families were friends. Their friend was extremely proud of his father. Our boys knew he loved them, too. He could not resist hugging them as if they were his own. He was very tall. If they happened to be standing in front of him he would bend down, reducing his height by more than half, to put his arm around them. To the boys it was nothing unusual. They were completely at home in his surrounding love. Since we were not actually related, if he was ever angry or distant in the privacy of his own family, our boys never knew about it. So to them he was a giant fortress of love.

Then one day he was bumped from an overbooked flight. Reluctantly yielding to a client's pressure that he be present at a meeting, for the first time in his life he hired a private plane. The plane crashed into a mountain and he was gone. To my sons it was shocking, stunning, horrible—an earthquake of tremendous proportions. That he was gone from their lives was heartrending. They felt the solid absence. And that a child could lose a father! that their friend had lost his! that they could lose theirs!—it was as if a hole had opened up on the bottom of the universe where you couldn't count on anything, where someone you love, or you yourself could fall through and be gone forever.

I waited with my friend, his wife, while they looked for the missing plane. We ironed his handkerchiefs, hoping, while we waited until word came. A hole *had* opened in the universe, and Martin had fallen through it. What it must have been for his family is beyond comprehension, because even for us it was enormous.

My two boys reacted differently. For days the younger one could not stop weeping. He'd be playing and having fun one minute, and the next I'd find him on our bed, awash in grief and fear. Mostly I just held him, and we cried together. What could I say? What did I know? But when the wave subsided and he asked for understanding, we groped together.

"Mom, it's so sad! It's so sad."

"It sure is. I don't know anything sadder."

"How could God let it happen?"

"I don't know. It is more than I can understand. There are some things in life that we can't understand."

I struggled to find something to assuage despair and to suggest hope. I did not want to say anything cheap. I could not say what I didn't know. And I did not know myself how to think about life and the falling through of people from right under your feet, Only tentatively did I finally offer my son the small life preserver of an idea that I have many times clung to myself.

"Don't you suppose that God will find new, different ways to love Eric? Martin was a wonderful way that God loved Eric. It must be that he will find new ways."

"Do you mean that he will get a new Daddy?"

"Maybe, I don't know. But it must be that God will find ways of being a father to Eric. Daddy is God's way of fathering you. Martin was God's way of fathering Eric."

Eric's grandmother was very much a part of Eric's family. She took the children on long vacations and often stayed with the family for extended periods of time. Because my mother-in-law lived in Holland, the children rarely saw her. My mother lived nearby, but was not into being a grandmother. On the other hand, our children had an amazing number of volunteer godparents who reached out to them with astonishing steadfast devotion and generosity.

"You know how Eric has such a good time with his grandmother?"

"Yes. She's great."

"Do your grandmothers spend much time with you?"

"No, I love Grandma, but I don't see her very often. And Oma is in Holland, so I never see her."

"But does Eric have a Sue or a Bob or a Leslie?"

"I don't think so."

"Maybe Sue and Bob and Leslie are God's way of being your grandmother."

My heart ached for him. I was so sorry for them to have to face this sad, weirdest fact of life—death—so early on. "I love my Daddy," he would cry, burying his face in my lap. It seemed too young to face this fear. There were no easy answers. We just held onto each other and felt for God.

As we went with the family through the traditional Jewish days of mourning, preparing the consolation meal and sitting shiva, our older boy showed little emotion and even worried aloud, "Why am I not sad?" It was just too huge to wrap his feelings around—like earthquake, famine, holocaust—until the funeral at the temple when he saw the coffin.

"Is Martin in that box?" he whispered.

"His body is," I said.

And sobbing, he turned into a little boy waterfall, pouring himself off the folding chair.

I admired, almost envied, my Jewish friends in those days because they seemed to know so beautifully what to do. There was a clear tradition for how to wade beside each other through the grief and back onto the beach of life. Everyone seemed to know what to do and what part to play. Food was brought by floods of friends and family. Friend by friend, family by family, with the rabbi presiding. The burden of anger, grief, fear was spread across many shoulders, the quest for God generously shared. Everyone seemed to understand: We would find God or go down together.

THE RUNAWAY BUNNY

Once there was a little bunny who wanted to run away.
So he said to his mother, "I am running away."
"If you run away," said his mother, "I will run after you. For you are my little bunny."

So begins *The Runaway Bunny,* a wonderful children's book by Margaret Wise Brown.

"If you run after me," said the little bunny, "I will become a fish in a trout stream and I will swim away from you."

"If you become a fish in a trout stream," said his mother, "I will become a fisherman and I will fish for you."

So the bunny keeps changing into things and the mother keeps changing into whatever matches his new form. My favorite is when he changes into a bird (still looking suspiciously like a rabbit) and she becomes, "a tree that you come home to." (She's a very rabbity tree.)

Portnoy's complaint? A child haunted by his mother? I don't think so, and like all of Margaret Wise Brown's stories, we found this one amazingly reassuring and peaceful. To me it is archetypal, a myth that deals with a very big question of both parent and child. When they are snuggled up side by side with a book, life together is so safe and good. Sooner or later the question arises in the hearts of both parent and child, what will happen if we get separated? What will happen to me if—when!—through growing up or growing old one of us goes away—or dies?

The answer this book suggests to both parent and child is that the same love that took shape in a baby bunny's life as a loving mother bunny and that takes shape in the mother's life as a lovable baby bunny to care for—that same love will take new shape when things change. No matter how bad you are or how far you go, the love you need will follow you all the days of your life. No matter how things change, your purpose, value, usefulness will follow you all the days of your life. You can never be lost. You will never be valueless. There is a parent beyond the parent for both parent and child. This book reminds me of a psalm:

> Whither shall I go from thy spirit?
> Or whither shall I flee from thy presence?
> If I ascend up into heaven, thou art there;
> If I make my bed in Sheol, behold, thou art there;
> If I take the wings of the morning
> and dwell in the uttermost parts of the sea,
> Even there shall thy hand lead me,
> And thy right hand shall hold me.
>
> —Ps. 139:7–10

WHAT CHANGES AND
WHAT DOESN'T

I happened to teach a fourth-grade Sunday-school class in the same month that the father of a teenager in the church died. So we spoke of *The Runaway Bunny* and how each new shape of God's love is just as good as the old, how in fact the old would not be as good. Is it good for an unborn baby to be in its mother? Is it good for the baby to come out? Yes. Would it be good for the baby to go back into the mother? No! Is it good when a baby can ride in a stroller instead of a carriage? Would it be better to ride in a stroller than to walk and run or ride a bike as you do? We talked of how the perfect shape for God's love to take in a little bunny's life is a big mother rabbit full of milk. But when he grows up and becomes a sailor or a pilot, would it be good for him to have a big mother rabbit full of milk? Ha ha. No. Ridiculous. Embarrassing! Yucky! they said.

I told them that my father had recently died and asked if they thought I still needed a father. Looking at my big gray-haired self they weren't too sure. So I told them that I sure do. I don't need God to take shape as a Daddy to pick me up and help me to walk and read bedtime stories any more. But I still need someone to take care of me and protect and love me and tell me what to do. Finding the new shape of God's love for us is what prayer is all about.

WHO CALLED?

When I came home, after hello, I always asked the same question.

"Any messages?"

"Yes," he said.

"Oh, no," I would say, judging by the look in his eye. "Not again. I mean really. Did anyone call?"

"Yes."

"Okay," I'd say, surrendering to the twinkle in his eye. "Who called?"

"Job," he'd say. "He wants to know the meaning of suffering."

It was a wonderful, awful, hilarious game in which the turning point of our seventeen-year-old parent/child relationship was acknowledged, made light of, and hopefully just in the nick of time, welcomed. I hated it. I loved it. It killed and inspired me. We had always had two relationships: human and divine. One stumbling and normal, the other spiritual and transcendent. The first was ending. From the beginning it was always ending. But lately everything had been telling us to let go. Undoubtedly he always would have. Through the grace of God and prayer occasionally we had. But now the time left in which to willingly let go for good was short. For years already I had been hurrying to let go, just to avoid the rope burn. But there was very little time left and still much letting go to occur. Unless we hurried and relinquished our parent/child tie and welcomed our true status as divine brother and sister, the next months, even years, would be hell. His jokes helped us.

"Mary called," he said. "She wants to know if you're willing to bear the next messiah."

So he mocked me—and it, easing himself—and me, free.

HOLY MOSES

Once I kicked my son.

Until today I have I have never told anyone this. It haunts me and fills me with shame. But now that he is grown, I think I am ready. Maybe it is something I can say; maybe I have to say it, like the Ancient Mariner, in public.

He was not yet nearly four feet tall when I kicked him. I didn't loft him into the air. I didn't knock him down. I don't think I even bruised him because I kicked him in the rear. But I did kick him through a doorway. He had been doing something to his little brother, and I was so angry—I can feel my jaw clenching. I was not sending him to his room. I was chasing him. Anger at whatever he had done and fear that he had had to do it just swelled until my foot popped out and kicked him.

I think my very deep sympathetic feeling for Moses was born in that moment—Moses who was so outraged by the wrong of an Egyptian beating up on a Hebrew that he killed the Egyptian. Oh, poor Moses. I know just how he felt. Since then I knew I didn't belong in the Promised Land either.

When he was nineteen, my victim's worst memory of himself from those days was that once when he was really angry he put his little brother's stuffed animals in the toilet. He recalled that he thought he would feel good, but as soon as they sank he felt terrible. "It still bothers me," he said. "Then I made him promise that he wouldn't tell. And he didn't, which made me feel even worse."

He happened to call while I was writing this. So I even confessed the horrible memory to him. He laughed and said he didn't remember being kicked. He did remember the stuffed animals. "But do you remember when I killed the spider that was killing the fly?" he said. I didn't.

"I saw the spider killing the fly and I thought it was so horrible that I killed the spider. As soon as I had done it I felt so terrible that I cried and cried. I felt guilty for a long time because I knew the spider was just doing what spiders are supposed to do. I couldn't stand to watch him kill the fly. And then I couldn't stand it that I had killed the spider."

He feels sorry for Moses, too.

So now I have told you the worst thing that I am going to tell you. It is not the worst thing that could be told, but it is a bad thing that was hard to tell. I hope it is somewhat comforting. You are not alone. More than once I have listened to parents say, "I knew it wouldn't always be great, but I never thought I would hate my child. And sometimes I do."

Everybody wants to know if the approach to child-rearing in *Whole Child/Whole Parent* worked. This is silly because it isn't a book about how to do it right, but about how to survive and how to get the full benefit and even some joy that family life brings. In that sense it worked. There was much learning, many blessings, and much joy. But if they mean, Was it all good? Was I a good parent? Were the children without problems? Did they turn out right? I can say yes and I can say no, I can laugh, and I can cry. The kicking episode I told you was not the worst. The death of our friend was not the worst. I will not tell you the worst—the overhanging threat to our lives, the ongoing failures to be loving. The rampant ignorance. The baffling concerns. I will only tell you that we had our share.

My husband is a horticulturist. In those days my horticulturist husband worked in a plant nursery. It takes tons of fertilizer, including a lot of manure, to feed the plants and make them grow. I was more involved with the children's nursery, and there was plenty of manure there too. If our sons are robust maybe it is because of, not in spite of, all the manure they had to grow in. There is plenty that simply stank. Maybe that's why they both grew so tall. It's a comforting theory anyway. It's my fertilizer theory.

I have my Utah theory, too. It says that everybody is born and grows up somewhere. Wherever you and your family live there is weather, some good and some bad. It is different from the good and bad weather in other parts of the country. You have some good that others have bad. You have bad that others have good. But everybody has both. And everybody in your family will have to contend with the same bad weather because you live in the same place. All members of your family also suffer from and have to learn to deal with the same mental climate.

Then there is the psycho ward theory. Everybody in any given family is from the same psycho ward as the rest of the family. All the members of one family are nuts in roughly the same way. We share and pass on to our children the same overriding delusions about who we are and what is important in life. So you can't compare yourselves to other families and say that you are better or worse. They may not have your problems; they have others. When our delusions give us problems we all use the same delusions to try to solve the problems. Things get worse and worse, until somebody gets desperate enough to go to God. That's what happened to Moses. Eventually he got so exasperated with his people that he went up on the mountain and got the Ten Commandments. But still he wasn't ready, and when he came down and saw everybody misbehaving he smashed the commandments, which only goes to show that he still didn't know what the power was that wasn't people overpowering each other. He was close. He understood the problem. He had received the answer. But he still hadn't understood it. He had to climb the mountain again, alone.

Somewhere in here I find a way to get to sleep at night and to go on with the business of spiritual growth and to continue to be sure that God is there. My son can laugh, so I can too. I hope you can. I believe each family is a petal opening, each generation is part of the petal. It is one petal in the great opening flower of human consciousness. Our problems are not our shame; they are our work. Each of us has certain work to do to grow beyond the generation before us. Not only for ourselves and our children but for the whole flower. Beyond us, below, are deep roots into truth. Beyond us, above, is the light of love. We are trying so hard, and we can't do it; it is all happening by grace, and we can't stop it.

POLLY BERRIEN BERENDS is a spiritually oriented psychotherapist who has lectured, taught, and led workshops at many institutes, churches, and schools in the United States. Her adult books *Whole Child/Whole Parent, Gently Lead: How to Teach Your Children About God While Finding Out for Yourself,* and *Coming to Life: Traveling the Spiritual Path in Everyday Life* reflect her lifelong personal journey and over twenty-five years as a therapist and parent. She is widely acclaimed for her ability to reveal the connection between spiritual truth and everyday practical concerns. Berends is a graduate of Union Theological Seminary with training in Jungian analysis and existential psychotherapy, and has done additional advanced studies in psychiatry and religion at Union Theological Seminary and the New School for Social Research. She lives in Hastings-on-Hudson, New York.